FABRICATING TECHNIQUES

Create It Yourself

Ken Voze

The Complete Street Machine Library™

Fabricating Techniques

Create It Yourself

Printed in 2006.

Published by National Street Machine Club under license from MBI Publishing Company.

Tom Carpenter
Creative Director

Heather Koshiol
Managing Editor

Jenya Prosmitsky
Book Design and Production

Jen Weaverling
Senior Book Development Coordinator

1 2 3 4 5 6 / 10 09 08 07 06

ISBN 1-58159-291-4

National Street Machine Club
12301 Whitewater Drive
Minnetonka, MN 55343
www.streetmachineclub.com

About the Author

After more than twenty-five years experience in film and television as an editor, writer, producer and director, **Ken Vose** made the transition to full time author in 1985. Vose, who lives in a small village in northeastern Pennsylvania, has written for *Motor Books International*, *International Auto Style & Sport*, *Millimeter*, *Super Car & Classics* and *Cigar Aficionado* magazines, and hosted *The Driver's Seat*, a syndicated television show. Ken was guest curator for the exhibition *Fantasy and Fins: The Artist and the Automobile* at the Petersen Museum in Los Angeles.

Contents

Introduction

What are the critical activities encompassed by the wonderful word "Fabricate"? Construct, manufacture, build, assemble, fashion, figure and form are all processes that are included. Invent, create, formulate and design also come to mind. All that pretty much seems to cover the gamut of the dictionary's description of the word.

While we can't promise that after reading the book you'll be able to construct the next Indy 500 winner or resurrect the oldest heap in the junkyard, we can promise that you'll be better informed about the entire fabrication process. Your fabricating skill levels and confidence in using them will also be ratcheted up several notches so that you can start to complete some of your own fabricating projects.

Fabricating Techniques will show you how to accomplish the task at hand with up-to-date information on using the best equipment and techniques to execute your project. In addition, there are many insider tips from a variety of fabrication pros. They're happy to share the knowledge and techniques they've gained in their experience, which you can adapt to your own projects. The fabricators included here may come from diverse backgrounds and may be decades apart in age, but they all have at least one thing in common: They learned their amazing

Fabricate/fabrikayt/v. construct, manufacture, build, erect, frame, raise, put up, set up, assemble, fashion, figure, form, make, produce, invent, create, originate, devise, formulate, design, hatch, think up.

skills by watching others, asking questions, and engaging in trial and error and some good old-fashioned hard work.

Three of the self-taught fabricators featured in this book have taken the fabrication concept to a level that boggles the mind. Although their stories might be categorized more as "see what you can do" rather than "see how you can do it," they are perfect examples of what can be accomplished when you refuse to believe that it can't be done.

The first, Rick Dobbertin, turned his dream of building an oceangoing amphibious vehicle into reality when he drove/sailed his converted milk tank truck to South America via the Caribbean Island chain. Now if that isn't a huge project, what is? He also is currently in the final stages of construction of his newest amphibious vehicle, the HydroCar.

Then, California hot rodder Al Teague gives insight on how he built a racing streamliner in a tiny garage with just some basic hand tools, an air compressor, a drill press, a reciprocating saw, an oxyacetylene welder, and a torch set. He eventually took the completed car to the Bonneville Salt Flats and set a world land speed record, blasting across the salt at more than 400 miles per hour.

Finally, Eddie Paul, who has built everything from movie stunt autos to aircraft to military lasers, describes in fascinating detail the process of building a mechanical great white shark that makes the fish in *Jaws* look like a large rubber bath toy.

In a world that places increasingly more emphasis on technology and higher education, these craftsmen stand apart. They actually get their hands dirty building pretty amazing stuff. And while architects and engineers are heralded for the design of their latest bridge or building, those structures really are only as strong as their weakest weld. In fact, because of the continued construction of everything from large skyscrapers to custom-designed products, those with strong fabrication skills are likely to be in demand in the workforce for years to come. As Los Angeles Trade Technical College welding professor Lisa Legohn simply puts it: "A great welder will always have a job."

Another recent development detailed in this book is how designing and machining custom mechanical parts can now be done online, thanks to people like Jim Lewis, who created the software and a website easy enough for a mass audience to use. His company estimates that it reduces the engineering and administrative time for a single custom part from 40 hours to only 15 minutes. "Although not as fast, it's almost like the transporter in *Star Trek*," Lewis says. Read on, and we'll put that notion to the test.

Also profiled are fabricators like Jerry Bowers, who helped craft both a hot rod school bus and racing wheelchair; Mark Carpenter, a box truck wrestling ring builder; and Eric Scarlett, who helped create a Porsche golf collector. Then more tips come from Renee Newell, a longtime welder and sculptor; Joe Barnes, a do-it-yourself race car builder; Ed Federkeil, a custom pickup truck builder; Dwaine Jungen, future off-road fabrication maestro; and Todd Blandford, a hydraulics expert.

Put it all together and what do you have? The auto world's definitive guide to *Fabricating Techniques*. Now, it's time to get wrenching.

Shop Setup And Basic Tools

It's up to you how easy a project will be. All you need are the right tools and a work space that's set up properly. Here's your guide.

A well-set-up shop is key to doing good work. You don't need a ton of space, but you will need the right equipment.

"A man can't have enough tools."
— Eddie Paul, Hollywood car builder

When it comes to setup, no fabrication shop is the same. If you plan, as Eddie Paul does, to be able to build a hundred movie cars in a month, as well as craft V-8 motorcycles, mechanical horses, and sharks, you'll need a lot of space—and everything from a Phillips screwdriver to full 3-D AutoCad capability. But if you plan to work on one car (or maybe one bus) at a time, you'll need a space to actually get the project done.

The garage is probably the most typical place for a shop, and if you have an extra-deep garage or a spare bay, you are in luck. If you don't, but have some space on your property, adding a small room onto the back or side of your garage is a possibility. Or if you are handy at all, you can pay someone to pour a slab and frame up the room, and you can do the Sheetrocking 'tend finish work. This is going to be a shop after

all—if your finishing skills are subpar, life goes on. You aren't going to be entertaining dinner guests out there!

If you are pouring a fresh slab and have to deal with cooler weather, consider in-floor heating. For a shop, it is ideal. The system circulates fluid through hoses in the concrete, and the warm floor is comfortable to work on. Using this kind of heat can be quite efficient, particularly if you use an electric on-demand water heater.

For those who don't have a garage or space for one, a basement or spare room is another possible location for your shop. The walk-out basement can be a decent place to build your shop, though you have to be wary of generating fumes and noise pollution into the above portion of the house.

The amount of space required for your shop will vary quite a bit, depending on your needs. Simply setting up in a corner of the garage, with a workbench, good light, ample outlets, and clever use of space, can be enough to do simple projects. If you are going to use larger equipment, such as welders, lathes, and sheet metal brakes, you will need more space to work with. Consider one stall of your garage, about 400 square feet, as a great starting place for an advanced shop. Also bear in mind that you will nearly always fill whatever space you create.

The best way to figure out the amount of space you need is to carefully draw up a plan for your shop. Place all the equipment you'll need in it, and be sure to allow ample work space around each tool. This method isn't foolproof, but it will help you figure out how much space is enough.

When setting up a shop, you are going to need plenty of electrical power. In a typical garage, 100-amp service is normally plenty of juice, even if you have a 220-volt outlet or two. If you are using a power-hungry combination of lifts, hoists, in-floor heating, or multiple welders, you may need more power. The key is identifying what kind of equipment you are going to be using, so lay out a map for where each piece goes (there's that layout again); and then calculate your electrical needs.

Another key to setting up a good working shop is to properly light it. You can't do quality work if you can't see what you are doing. Sounds pretty basic, but you'd be surprised how many shops look like something out of the dark ages. Keep in mind that the type of lighting is less important than the quality. In other

words, whether it's natural, fluorescent, direct, indirect, or whatever, it needs to clearly illuminate the work areas that are to be used, ideally to the point of eliminating shadows entirely if possible.

Here's an area where auxiliary lighting is a great help and is economical. Portable light banks are available at home improvement stores for less than $50, and they are ideal for working on projects in which overhead light doesn't suffice (when working under the hood of your car, for example).

Expert fabricator Rick Dobbertin says he uses a lot of fluorescent lighting in his shop. "Set the light banks up with three or four switches in a way that you don't always have to have every light on all the time," he says. "This will save on the bulbs and the electricity. Sometimes I'll work all day and never turn anything on except the lights over the workbench."

Placement of outlets is another key point in planning your shop setup. You'll want lots of outlets near the workbench(es) and on the walls in work spaces. Bear in mind that you'll want to be able to use welders and other electrical equipment in any part of the shop.

The physical location of your shop equipment, tools, workbench, storage facilities, and so on should be decided upon before you move everything in rather than after. A good workbench is one of the single most important items in your shop. If space permits, you might even consider having two of them, one made of wood with locking casters so you can move it around the shop and the other of metal, which can be used for welding, hammering, or other heavy work. Also don't forget to bolt a vise securely to one corner of the table.

Tools

A toolbox and a complete set of brand-name tools, both metric and standard, is another essential part of setting up your shop. Buying a fairly comprehensive basic set will cost between $200 and $700, and the lower-priced 150-or-so-piece set is a good starting point for beginners. Higher-end tools will cost you quite a bit more. They are a bit nicer to work with, but are a hard expense to jus-

Having the right tools is the key to setting up a good shop. They don't need to be the latest, most expensive tools to do the job, either.

tify unless you work with your tools 40 hours a week.

If you have time on your hands, you can find used tools for less. Hand tools can be found everywhere from your local hardware store to flea markets and garage sales. Don't turn your back on some of the bargains to be found in non-traditional outlets.

HydroCar builder Rick Dobbertin has had good luck picking up more expensive tools at swap meets, and he's not afraid to work with unknown brands. "Proper tools don't have to mean expensive tools," he says. "I like having multiple tools of the same thing. I have five air die grinders, each set up with a different tool; a couple of carbide burrs; a bunch of C-clamps (from 2 inch to 10 inch); a sanding disc; a barrel sander; and a polisher. It saves time not having to change the heads every couple of minutes. I bought all five air grinders for under $50 about 10 years ago. They all still work. With proper care, the cheap stuff will work for years."

Recommended Hand Tool List

The following is a list of the tools every fabricator should have in his or her shop:

¼-inch drive socket set

- 4-millimeter 6-point socket
- 5-millimeter 6-point socket
- 6-millimeter 6-point socket
- 7-millimeter 6-point socket
- 8-millimeter 6-point socket
- 9-millimeter 6-point socket
- 10-millimeter 6-point socket
- 11-millimeter 6-point socket
- 12-millimeter 6-point socket
- 13-millimeter 6-point socket
- ³⁄₁₆-inch 6-point deep socket
- ⁷⁄₃₂-inch 6-point deep socket
- ¼-inch 6-point deep socket
- ⁹⁄₃₂-inch 6-point deep socket
- ⁵⁄₁₆-inch 6-point deep socket
- ¹¹⁄₃₂-inch 6-point deep socket
- ³⁄₈-inch 6-point deep socket
- ⁷⁄₁₆-inch 6-point deep socket
- ½-inch 6-point deep socket
- ⁹⁄₁₆-inch 6-point deep socket
- Quick-release ratchet
- 1½-inch extension bar
- 3-inch extension bar

³⁄₈-inch drive socket set

- 9-millimeter 12-point socket
- 10-millimeter 12-point socket
- 11-millimeter 12-point socket
- 12-millimeter 12-point socket
- 13-millimeter 12-point socket
- 14-millimeter 12-point socket
- 15-millimeter 12-point socket
- 16-millimeter 12-point socket
- 17-millimeter 12-point socket
- 18-millimeter 12-point socket
- 19-millimeter 12-point socket
- 9-millimeter 6-point deep socket
- 10-millimeter 6-point deep socket
- 11-millimeter 6-point deep socket
- 12-millimeter 6-point deep socket
- 13-millimeter 6-point deep socket
- 14-millimeter 6-point deep socket
- 15-millimeter 6-point deep socket
- 16-millimeter 6-point deep socket
- 17-millimeter 6-point deep socket
- 18-millimeter 6-point deep socket
- 19-millimeter 6-point deep socket
- ³⁄₈-inch 12-point standard socket
- ⁷⁄₁₆-inch 12-point standard socket
- ½-inch 12-point standard socket
- ⁹⁄₁₆-inch 12-point standard socket
- ⁵⁄₈-inch 12-point standard socket
- ¹¹⁄₁₆-inch 12-point standard socket
- ¾-inch 12-point standard socket
- ¹³⁄₁₆-inch 12-point standard socket
- ³⁄₈-inch 6-point deep socket
- ⁷⁄₁₆-inch 6-point deep socket
- ½-inch 6-point deep socket
- ⁹⁄₁₆-inch 6-point deep socket

In addition to the right tools, you should have plenty of small containers on hand for parts, bolts, and materials. Old plastic food containers and coffee cans are great catchalls.

Specialty tools, like this drill press, are great items to find at swap meets, flea markets, and garage sales.

- $5/8$-inch 6-point deep socket
- $11/16$-inch 6-point deep socket
- $3/4$-inch 6-point deep socket
- $13/16$-inch 6-point deep socket
- $7/8$-inch 6-point deep socket
- $5/32$-inch hex bit socket
- $13/16$-inch hex bit socket
- $7/32$-inch hex bit socket
- $1/4$-inch hex bit socket
- $5/16$-inch hex bit socket
- $3/8$-inch hex bit socket
- $5/8$-inch 6-point spark plug socket
- $13/16$-inch 6-point spark plug socket
- Quick release ratchet
- 3-inch extension bar
- 6-inch extension bar
- $3/8$-inch to $1/4$-inch adapter

$1/2$-inch drive socket set
- 12-millimeter 6-point standard socket
- 13-millimeter 6-point standard socket
- 14-millimeter 6-point standard socket
- 15-millimeter 6-point standard socket
- 16-millimeter 6-point standard socket
- 17-millimeter 6-point standard socket
- 18-millimeter 6-point standard socket
- 19-millimeter 6-point standard socket
- 20-millimeter 6-point standard socket
- 21-millimeter 6-point standard socket
- 22-millimeter 6-point standard socket
- 23-millimeter 6-point standard socket
- 24-millimeter 6-point standard socket
- 25-millimeter 6-point standard socket
- 26-millimeter 6-point standard socket
- 27-millimeter 6-point standard socket

- $3/8$-inch 6-point standard socket
- $7/16$-inch 6-point standard socket
- $1/2$-inch 6-point standard socket
- $9/16$-inch 6-point standard socket
- $5/8$-inch 6-point standard socket
- $11/16$-inch 6-point standard socket
- $3/4$-inch 6-point standard socket
- $13/16$-inch 6-point standard socket
- $7/8$-inch 6-point standard socket
- $15/16$-inch 6-point standard socket
- 1-inch 6-point standard socket
- $11/16$-inch 6-point standard socket
- $11/8$-inch 6-point standard socket
- $11/4$-inch 6-point standard socket
- $1/2$-inch to $3/8$-inch adapter
- Quick release ratchet
- 3-inch extension bar
- 6-inch extension bar

- Fluke multitester
- Safety glasses
- Universal spoke wrench
- Valve stem remover
- Scientific calculator
- Metric thread pitch gauge
- U.S. thread pitch gauge

Combination wrenches
- 6-millimeter combination wrench
- 7-millimeter combination wrench
- 8-millimeter combination wrench
- 9-millimeter combination wrench
- 10-millimeter combination wrench
- 11-millimeter combination wrench
- 12-millimeter combination wrench
- 13-millimeter combination wrench
- 14-millimeter combination wrench
- 15-millimeter combination wrench
- 16-millimeter combination wrench
- 17-millimeter combination wrench
- 18-millimeter combination wrench
- 19-millimeter combination wrench
- $1/4$-inch combination wrench
- $5/16$-inch combination wrench
- $11/32$-inch combination wrench
- $3/8$-inch combination wrench
- $7/16$-inch combination wrench
- $1/2$-inch combination wrench
- $9/16$-inch combination wrench
- $5/8$-inch combination wrench
- $11/16$-inch combination wrench
- $3/4$-inch combination wrench
- $13/16$-inch combination wrench
- $7/8$-inch combination wrench
- $15/16$-inch combination wrench
- $11/16$-inch combination wrench

Additional Hand Tools

Screwdrivers
- Phillips screwdriver #0
- Phillips screwdriver #1
- Phillips screwdriver #2
- Phillips screwdriver #3
- $3/16$ x 4-inch screwdriver
- $1/4$ x 6-inch screwdriver
- Posi-drive #1, 2, 3, 4
- Angle driver (for carb adjustment)

Pliers sets
- Sidecut
- Channel lock
- Hose clamp crimpers

$3/8$-inch T-handle

$3/8$-inch air ratchet

$3/8$-inch drive Allen sockets
- Straight and ball sockets (short and long)
- $3/16$-inch to $3/8$-inch sockets
- Long 5-millimeter socket

Crow's foot set
- $3/8$-inch to $1 1/8$-inch

Torx driver bit set
- Up to and including #40 and #45

Torque adapter set
- $3/8$-inch to $3/4$-inch
- $1/2$-inch extension sets
- 2-inch to 12-inch straight

Hand impact driver and bits

Air impact wrenches
- $3/8$-inch and $1/2$-inch

Torque wrenches (click type)
- $3/8$-inch to 288-inch pound
- $3/8$-inch to 75-inch pound
- $1/2$-inch to 288-inch pound

Line wrenches
- $1/4$-inch, $5/16$-inch, $3/8$-inch, $7/8$-inch

Crescent wrenches
- 10-inch and 12-inch

Complete set of metal files
- File handles
- Thread files
- Jewelers' files

A digital caliper is extremely useful for making precise measurements.

Feeler gauge (flat and wire type)

Others
- 6-inch adjustable wrench
- $3/4$-inch pliers with wire cutting slot (6)
- 6-inch long-nose pliers
- 7-inch adjustable joint pliers
- 20-piece hex key set
- $3/8$ x $4 1/2$-inch center punch
- $5/32$ x 5-inch pin punch
- $3/8$ x $4 1/2$-inch prick punch
- 6-piece impact driver set
- 16-ounce ball-peen hammer
- 36-blade master feeler gauge
- Tire gauge
- 13-piece balldriver hex key set
- Dead blow hammer
- $1/2$-inch needle-nose vise grips pliers (7)
- Wire cutter
- Channel locks
- Convertible retaining ring pliers
- Double-point scriber (2)
- Single-point scriber
- Safety glasses
- Drill bits (numbered, lettered, and fractional—all sizes to $1/2$-inch)
- Chemicals (contact cleaner, etc.)
- Hacksaw
- Assorted blades
- Tap and die set
- $1/2$-inch pneumatic drill
- Bolt cutters
- Automatic center punch
- Pop rivet gun

- Shop towels
- Flashlight
- Heavy vise

Electrical
- Digital multimeter (10-amp scale, 300-milliamp scale)
- Battery charger
- Timing light
- Charging system and battery
- Load tester
- Jumper leads (24 inches long)
- Three inductive ammeters (14 gauge with 30-amp clips)
- Test light

In addition to the standard hand tools, here are some more tools you should consider adding to your shop:

- MIG welder
- Drill press
- Chop saw
- Sawzall
- Air compressor
- Oxy torch
- Saber saw
- Plasma cutter
- Hand grinders
- Vise
- Reciprocating handsaw
- Hole saw
- Band saw
- Deburring tool
- Small lathe
- English wheel
- Tubing bender
- Sheet metal brake

- Shrinker/stretcher
- Sander
- Air hammer
- Nibbler
- Jack stands
- Clamps in various sizes
- Tap and die set
- Angle finder
- Level
- Framing square
- Straightedge
- Wire brushes
- Markers

This list is far from complete, given the range of available tools and equipment and the many different types of fabrication for which they were designed. Just remember you can always add tools as you need them, or when you decide whether you really need them or not.

Shop Safety

The most important part of setting up your shop is making it a safe place to work. "Don't attempt anything without the proper safety equipment because you never know what's going to happen," says Mark Carpenter, who helped build a box-truck wrestling ring. "By proper equipment I mean things like safety glasses, ear protection, leather work gloves, face shields, cutting goggles, welding helmets, welding jackets, cotton-blend clothing, a first aid kit, and a fire extinguisher." Rick Dobbertin seconds Carpenter's advice, adding: "Have at least one fully charged fire extinguisher handy. Something that took years to build could be gone in seconds if a single spark hits the wrong material."

Another aspect of shop safety is making sure your working area is well ventilated and clean, as well as free of flammable and combustible liquids and objects.

An angle grinder is an extremely useful tool for working metal. The tool is basically a portable grinding wheel, and it can be used to take off welding slag, round edges, and grind away most types of metal.

PLANNING YOUR PROJECT

While it's possible to guess your way through a project, chances are you'll end up with a mess. A good plan eliminates guesswork. Follow these simple guidelines.

"Plan your build, and build your plan."
— Rick Dobbertin, amphibious car builder

While the amount of planning needed to fabricate something like a simple automotive suspension bracket may be miniscule in comparison with that required for the fabrication of an entire suspension system, it does not make the process any less important. In fact, proper planning is the most important step in taking your project from concept to reality. You planned your shop setup based on the types of projects you intended to build there, now it's time to plan the projects themselves.

"One of the biggest mistakes beginning fabricators make is the lack of good planning," race car builder Joe Barnes says. "I've built race cars using a tape measure and a welder, putting things where I thought they should be, or where I'd seen them on other cars. Now I make fully drawn plans so that I know where everything is going to go and what the outcome will be."

The first step is to decide what your project is and set your goals accordingly. Some of the obvious questions you should be asking yourself in this step include the following:

- Do I have the right tools and equipment to do the job?
- How much is it going to cost, and can I afford it?
- How long will it take me?
- Do I have the skill level needed to do the job properly, or will I need help?

Once you start thinking about the project, you'll probably come up with a few more questions to add to that list.

"Then start by laying out your project—draw it, think about it, look at it, check your dimensions to make sure you haven't missed anything," master fabricator Mark Carpenter says. "Take your time. It takes a minute to weld a piece; it will take twice that to cut it out and replace it. That's what you will have to do if it's wrong—or just plain scrap it and start over."

Once you've worked on the project in your mind, now it's time to put those ideas on paper. Your "blueprint" can be as elaborate or rudimentary as you wish; whether it's done on your computer or the back of a paper napkin makes no difference, as long as it is sufficient to get the job done.

Probably the best, and most foolproof, way to lay out your project is by making a full-size drawing of the part you want to build. In other words, draw the part so that one inch on paper equals one inch on the finished metal part. This can be done with the simplest drafting tools: a ruler, compass, triangle, and so on, items that can be found anywhere school supplies are sold.

With this layout design, or pattern, you will be able to visualize the completed part—width, depth, height, angles, whatever—before you put tool to metal. Don't rush through this part of the fabrication process. Time spent getting the

pattern perfect is time well spent. The pattern itself can be drawn on plain or graph paper, or it can be drawn onto some sort of poster stock that can easily be used as a template to mark the metal that is to be shaped.

Many fabricators, as you will see, take the completed pattern and use it to make a cardboard mockup of the planned part, allowing them to visualize the part in 3-D without the aid, or expense, of CAD software.

"My approach when starting any project is to visualize, and sort of build it in my head as much as possible," hot rod bus builder Jerry Bowers says. "I go through each process, visualizing and doing accurate drawings. The rule of thumb is always measure twice, cut once. Actually, you can never measure too many times. That's where most people get it wrong, by not thinking it through

A typical work schedule at a small fabrication shop. The schedule doesn't have to be neat; it just has to do the job.

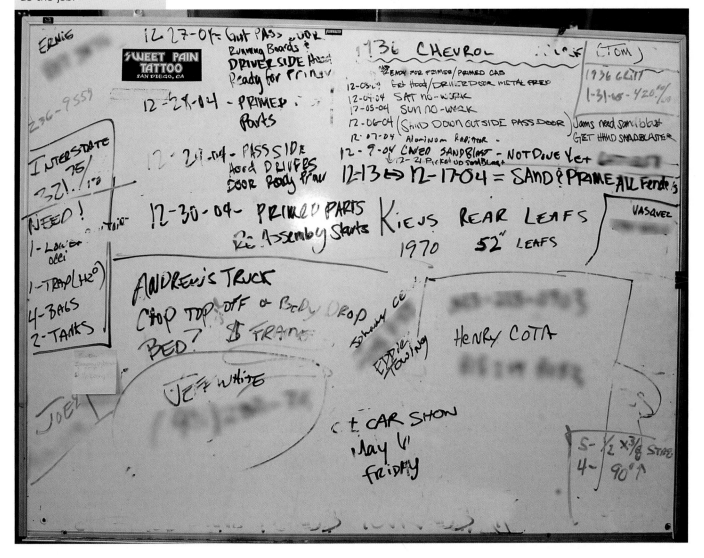

enough and not measuring enough."

Using your completed "blueprint," make a list of all the materials needed to finish the job: what kind of steel, the necessary hardware, special tools, or other equipment that you may have to buy or borrow. Once you've done that, you'll have a pretty good idea of how long the job will take and how much it is going to cost.

"Most big projects are what I call 'X' jobs," Dobbertin says. "You can estimate the time and the cost, then multiply that by two, or even three times, depending on the complexity, to get an idea of what you're really looking at. If you realize this up front, you won't go as crazy down the road. Planning ahead can save you a lot of time and money."

If you know someone who has done a project similar to the one you're contemplating, talk to them and find out if they encountered any unexpected difficulties, or discovered a shortcut that would work for you as well. If they happen to be more experienced with this type of job, ask if you can call on them for advice if you need it. Instructional books and videos also are great learning tools, but until someone comes up with the technology that will allow them to answer your questions, nothing beats the help of someone who's been there, done that.

"You don't have to go to school to learn how to do this stuff," says Al Teague. "Listen to people who know and they'll show you what you need to do. The more you work with it, the more you'll learn."

For certain types of projects, the final stage before you actually put a torch to metal is to make a template of the part out of paper, cardboard, and masking or duct tape. If the diamond that you visualized turns out to be a lump of coal, it's better to find out before you've started the fabrication rather than after.

"I buy 4x8-foot sheets of cardboard and I model everything with it first because it's so much easier to work with than trying to use metal," Dobbertin says.

If genius is, as they say, 90 percent perspiration and 10 percent inspiration, does it follow that fabrication is 90 percent mental and 10 percent metal? Probably not, but you never know for sure.

Percentages aside, the plain truth of the matter is that making a plan is at

With computer-aided drafting and online part design websites, your PC can help get your project nailed down to a T. *David Pruitt*

least as important a part of the fabrication process as is the physical process of cutting, bending, or welding.

Fabrication: Art or Craft?

The debate concerning just what separates fine art from craft has probably been going on since the days of the cavemen, when perhaps our ancestors who painted the cave walls tried to distance themselves from the guys in the tribe who made designer stone axes. In today's world, the definition is no less clear, as fine-arts sculptors regularly use techniques common to all metal fabricators. Some artists, like John Chamberlin, use parts found in automobile junkyards as the raw material for their works. Even New York's prestigious Museum of Modern Art includes a number of hand-crafted automobiles in its permanent collection.

For sculptors working with metal, the tools and techniques are essentially the same as those used by all of the fabricators included in this book. The answer to the art vs. craft debate is simple: fabrication is a craft that can, in the right hands, reach the level of art.

MEET THE PROS

Renee Newell

"For me, the love of metal came before welding."

Looking at the work of artist Renee Newell, the last thing that you'd be likely to think about is welding—a hot, grimy, industrial process that holds just about everything in our modern world together. Yet Renee is a certified industrial welder and a fine art sculptor . . . and admits to being fascinated with fire.

That's part of the reason she got into welding. "At campfires, I'm always the one tending the fire, making sure it's getting air," she says. "So when I first started to weld, it was like, WOW."

As an artist, she has sold numerous pieces, and as a welder, she has done her share of heavy-duty construction work. So she knows both disciplines well.

"There is a big difference between welding a piece of sculpture and doing commercial welding where you are essentially just running a bead," Newell says. "In structural welding, you're going to be putting down bead after bead, and it gets pretty monotonous. Whereas, in sculpture, you are creating. You're not just welding pieces together; you're manipulating the metal."

"For women artists out there who want to work with metal, I'll say that, to me, welding is easier for women," she adds. "I think because there is a certain rhythm involved and a need for patience. But for any artist, regardless of gender, who wants to get into metal sculpture, I'd tell them to get a small MIG machine, because anyone can learn to use it—just get a good instruction book with lots of pictures. Or, if not a MIG, then a little buzz box arc welder, and start with a low amperage drag rod like the E6013; it's easy to control and helps the novice welder to find their rhythm before starting to try and bite into the metal with an E7018."

Newell also suggests using an easy-to-form, easy-to-weld metal, so you won't have to worry about burning holes in the material. Of course, the best thing about metal is that if you do burn through it, you can always fix it. "You can put back what you've taken off," Newell says.

When done right, welding becomes more than a craft—it becomes an art, Newell adds. "But, as Lisa Legohn is fond of saying, it's not glamorous. Personally, I don't mind getting dirty, and if you want to weld, neither should you."

Renee Newell sees welding as art as much as craft and advises future welders to start with a simple MIG welding box and a good book.

SHEET METAL

W hether flat or shaped with compound curves, properly formed sheet metal can make the difference between an average job and a show-stopping work of art. Here's how to do it right.

Angle grinders are one of the basic tools of sheet metal work. They can grind just about any metal and are used for everything from smoothing bodywork to cutting off bolts.

"Metal is easier to cut than most people think. There are a lot of different tools for the job, but no one is right for every type of cut."
— Eddie Paul, Hollywood car builder

Two expert sheet metal fabricators really exemplify how different a sheet metal shop can be. Mark Carpenter's MTJ Manufacturing is a large operation, handling machining, fabrication, and assembly of components for commercial and industrial applications, as well as building vertical lifting systems for the material-handling markets. Jerry Bowers, on the other hand, fabricates one-off hot rods and the occasional school bus in his one-man operation.

Space

The size of your shop will determine to a great extent the type of work that can be accomplished inside it. Unless you are constructing a purpose-built building, you will have to make the best use of what you have.

MTJ occupies its own building that encompasses more than 10,000 square feet of space: a 4,700-square-foot shop with a 21-foot ceiling, a 3,200-square-foot shop with a 12- to 14-foot ceiling, and 2,400 square feet of office space. The shop includes a full complement of basic hand and power tools, four MIG welders, a TIG welder, a 400-amp arc welder, a plasma cutter, four band saws, a 65-ton iron worker, a 65-ton mechanical press brake, two lathes, two horizontal mills, two electric and one gas heat-treat ovens, a drill press, a nibbler, full auto-CAD capability, and, as they say in the commercials, "much, much more."

According to Carpenter, a 30x30-foot space is about as small as a practical sheet metal shop can be, although some sheet metal work can be done in a space as small as 16x16 feet, providing there is still room for a decent-sized workbench and a clear area around the work space of at least 3 feet.

The tools and equipment needed by Bowers (listed separately later in this chapter) in his 1,600-square-foot shop

Metal can be shaped and cut using a large grinding wheel. Consider your project before selecting your equipment.

obviously are but a fraction of what is available at Carpenter's shop. But, as Bowers puts it, most automotive sheet metal projects can be done in a space the size of a one-and-a-half to two-car garage, except for those pesky school bus builds.

So assuming you have a reasonably large, well-lit and well-ventilated space, what equipment will you need to do the job?

Equipment

Mark Carpenter recommends the following: basic hand tools, a chop saw, a sawzall, a band saw, a grinder, and a power drill. "For welding, it all depends [on] what you intend to use it for—sheet metal, tubing, small structural, whatever," he says. "Years ago, a gentleman I worked with making filter tanks told me when I was getting ready to expand my shop that I had to make up my mind if I was going to do sheet metal or plate and then buy the appropriate equipment to go that way. I set up for sheet metal and it works fine for everything in 10-gauge or lighter. If I need anything heavier bent, I have to send it out."

Doing any metal fabrication job by hand requires the proper hand tools. In order to "measure twice, cut once," you'll need any of the following: a selection of steel rulers of varying lengths, a retractable tape measure, framing squares, and a combination square set. You'll also want a center punch and a metal compass, or divider, for scribing arcs and circles. After the measuring comes the cutting.

The most commonly used hand-cutting tools are tin snips for making straight line cuts and aviation snips for cutting curved lines. Electric or pneumatic hand shears for cutting heavier steel and a power drill with a hole saw attachment could also be considered essential items.

"It's helpful to have two or three vises, six-inch to eight-inch, at least one with a swivel head," expert fabricator Rick Dobbertin says. "You'll need hammers, chisels, lots of standard and metric box and open-ended wrenches, screwdrivers, pliers, vise grips, and every size and shape of file that you can find."

When it comes to power tools, Mark Carpenter recommends these:

A chop saw: A lightweight (about 30 pounds) portable circular saw. Can be a miter chop saw for wood, with a blade for cutting aluminum.

A Sawzall: A reciprocating saw for cutting pipe and plate.

A band saw: Stationary or handheld, it makes more accurate, dedicated cuts than the Sawzall.

A disc grinder: Stationary or handheld, it removes bad welds, rust, or paint, and works for deburring rough edges.

A die grinder: Deburrs rough edges, grinds down metal to size, and cleans up welds.

A power drill: Makes starter holes for hole saws, installation of hardware, and so on.

Of all the cutting tools available none is more versatile, or makes a cleaner, more professional-looking cut than the plasma cutter. This is the Superman of cutting tools because it is able to cut through a 1/2-inch steel plate as if it were butter and in just about any way you desire. Plasma cutters "cut" by sending pressurized gas through a small channel that holds a negatively charged electrode. When the tip of the cutter touches metal, it creates a circuit that causes a spark that heats the gas, turning it into 30,000 degrees Fahrenheit plasma, which then turns metal molten. Although they are somewhat expensive, plasma cutters are cleaner and easier to use than most other cutting methods.

"The first time I picked one up, I was cutting through steel like it was paper," Eddie Paul says. "I've used them for years; they're fast and easy to use once

you get the hang of not quite touching the tip of the cutter to the metal. You have to work with it about a quarter of an inch away."

If you're planning to do larger jobs that hand tools alone can't handle, the most obvious piece of equipment you'll need is a sheet metal brake, which is used to bend and cut large sheets of metal. Sheet metal brakes come in a variety of sizes, but the most practical for a small shop is one about eight feet long, as this will handle standard full-sized sheets of metal. Because sheet metal brakes are large and relatively expensive pieces of equipment, it is worthwhile to look for a good used one, preferably a "combination" brake, which will allow you to make multiple bends at angles to each other rather than be restricted to the parallel bends of the standard sheet metal brake.

There are, of course, other large types of sheet metal–forming equipment, including shears and rollers, but they go beyond the scope of what we are discussing here. As we noted earlier, take the time to be sure of what it is that you want to accomplish in the shop and select your equipment accordingly.

Chop saws provide a square cut of metal stock, which is particularly useful when building anything that has butt joints.

OUT IN THE GARAGE

BUILDING A PORTABLE TOOL CADDY

When we asked Mark Carpenter to think of a project that could be accomplished by someone with a good basic fabrication setup, he came up with something that's not only functional but, as you'll see, eye-catching as well: a portable toolbox/welding caddy.

Although Carpenter based the idea for the toolbox caddy on the ones used by race car mechanics in the pits at the track, this one is intended for use in the shop on a concrete floor. The first step was to decide on the size of the unit. Carpenter wanted to include a toolbox he received, but he also wanted a large, double-size box as well.

When installing the toolbox, make sure to anchor it to the cart by bolting the bottom of the box to the cart frame. When moving the cart, make sure it is on solid level ground, the tanks are secure, regulators are protected, and the drawers are locked.

You might remember Carpenter's earlier comment about the unit being open and not covered in sheet metal. Well, Carpenter being Carpenter, once he looked at the completed unit, he decided it deserved to be diamond plated.

"When someone asks, 'Where did you get it from?' you can say, 'I made it.' And that is what it's all about," Carpenter says. "I feel that way about every piece of equipment that goes out of my shop."

1

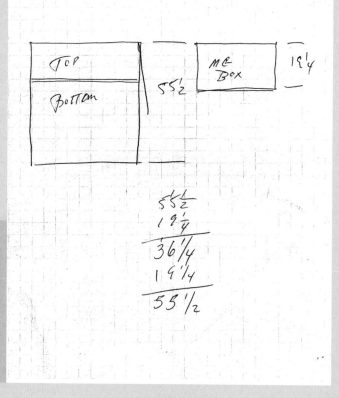

1: After obtaining the measurements of a larger box, Carpenter made his design sketches for the portable tool caddy. "The unit was obviously going to be heavy, so I knew we'd need large casters since the larger diameter of the wheels would make it easier to roll around," he says. The sketches were drawn freehand and at first Carpenter wanted to put the MIG welder and welding gas tank on one end and oxy and acetylene tanks on the other. But he realized the cart would then be unstable. So in the end, he added a large box with a storage area underneath the existing toolbox, which would house the MIG machine, a welding helmet, a hydraulic jack, and jack stands. *Mark Carpenter*

2: One of Carpenter's metal workbenches with some of the tools to be used in the build. These include: an electronic welding helmet, safety glasses, welding gloves, cutting goggles, heavy work gloves, a 48-inch T-Square, a 16-inch adjustable square, bar clamps, a hammer and tape measure, framing squares (large & small), a grinder, a drill, a $1/4$-inch air/hydraulic riveter, a marker and striker, magnetic clamps, C-clamps, and reference photos. *Mark Carpenter*

3: To save time on the project, Carpenter used a large-capacity automatic mitering saw to make 45-degree angle cuts on the tube ends for the cart frame. These can be cut with a chop saw, porta-band, or Sawzall, or you can cut the tubes square and deduct for the tube thickness, then buy matching-size plastic insert caps to plug up the ends of the tubes. *Mark Carpenter*

4: When you're laying out the base of the frame, you should always double-check your dimensions and make sure everything is square. *Mark Carpenter*

5: When squaring up the frame, tack the corners after you have made both sides parallel and the corners square by measuring diagonally. Both diagonal lengths should be the same. Use the bottom frame as a template so you don't have to continually spend extra time setting up each frame. The bottom frame is the jig—from there it's like stacking building blocks. *Mark Carpenter*

6: Use a small adjustable square to stack the upper frame sections and make sure they are even with the sides of the template frame. *Mark Carpenter*

7: Here are three frame uprights stacked on the template frame, showing how easily these pieces can be "mass produced." *Mark Carpenter*

8: Based on the concept drawings of your layout, mark the edge of the frame for the location of the toolbox partitions, just like laying out studs when framing in construction. Carpenter put a line on the lower frame for location of the vertical frame's edge and an X on the side of the line the frame would go on. *Mark Carpenter*

9: Using the marks for reference, check everything with a tape measure or ruler. When you're dealing with steel tubing, you don't want to have to move it an inch this way and then back again. "Get your reference mark, then double-check it," Carpenter says. "You're not covering this with sheet metal—it's all open, so everything needs to be right on the money." *Mark Carpenter*

10

11

10: If you're doing a project like this by yourself, you'll want to get some clamps or magnetic holding devices to help keep the metal vertical. If using magnetic devices, don't use any that are rated under the weight of the object you are trying to hold in place. And when you're working on something overhead, use a clamp. "They're not cheap; [they] can be as much as $50 or more each, but they sure help," Carpenter says. *Mark Carpenter*

11: This cast-steel clamp (not cast iron, which is not recommended) is cut in half and welded to the metal workbench. It's used to lock the frame securely in place. *Mark Carpenter*

12: Laying out the back side of the cart where the three gas tanks will go. Two $^1/_4$ x 4-inch plates welded flush to the bottom of the lower tubes (one piece with tank separators on top) of the frame will support the tanks. The frame is double-reinforced to handle the weight. *Mark Carpenter*

13: With the magnets holding everything in place, use a small, or adjustable, steel square to make sure everything is positioned equally and square. *Mark Carpenter*

14: The three upright frames in place. *Mark Carpenter*

15: The frame, now freestanding and tacked together. A straightedge and long bar clamps keep everything correctly positioned. Before you cut the horizontal tubes that separate the top of the frame, you should always measure from the point where they attach to the base frame. You should measure from the bottom first and cut the tube to match the bottom piece. "Once you get everything all squared at the top, take your bar clamps and get it square in multiple directions," Carpenter says. "I use what I call sacrificial tubing. The tube is tacked into place on the front with small welds, which will help control the warping, on one edge only, so that nothing moves while I'm welding in all of the smaller pieces. When you're finished, just break it off with a wrench by pulling back against the welds." *Mark Carpenter*

16: After welding metal, you should wait until it is well cooled before you check to see if it is warped. If it is, go back with a torch to correct it. "For example, if you welded two inches, you heat two inches on the opposite side area . . . and heat the metal until it is cherry red," Carpenter says. "Move the torch to keep the metal cherry red for the distance of the weld—it should straighten and will equalize." *Mark Carpenter*

17: With the toolboxes in place, check to see how they fit and how it will look. *Mark Carpenter*

18: "I like to weld everything, but casters I design to be bolted into place. Six-inch casters will work best," Carpenter says. "There are two swivel casters and two rigid casters, so it can be steered, and all of them have brakes and 200-pound-load capacity each. Don't buy cheap casters. If they collapse and the unit falls over, it'll be a real mess. Always remember, when you roll the unit around you have to lock the toolbox drawers—otherwise, when you go around a corner . . ." *Mark Carpenter*

19: Circles equal to the diameter of the gas tanks are cut into $^3/_{16}$-inch plate, with a 36-inch radius capacity nibbler. A cutting torch, reciprocating saw, or saber saw with a bi-metal blade will also work. They are sheared down the center to create the separating half moons. *Mark Carpenter*

20: A view of the finished product from the back. *Mark Carpenter*

EMBOSSED FLAMES

When asked to consider a project for the do-it-yourself rodder with good basic equipment, Jerry Bowers immediately focused on one of the new trends in the rod and tuner world: embossed flames on interior door panels. In fact, he now plans to make similar panels for installation on the pickup.

Depending on the vehicle, flames can be painted or airbrushed onto the panel or, in the case of Bowers' pickup, be left a single color. Leaving them one color more effectively highlights the embossed area.

"A plasma cutter would have worked to cut the flames, but I prefer to use a quality-built reciprocating hand jigsaw," he says. "I've been doing it this way for many years with good results, and it leaves a smooth, even cut line. I also feel I have more control over the project I'm working on. This interior door panel project took me approximately eight hours, and the total cost of material was approximately $150."

Using the right tools for the job at hand is also important. If you're just setting up, Bowers suggests getting what he has in his shop:

- A MIG welder
- Basic air tools
- A large air compressor
- A good reciprocating hand saw
- A Sawzall
- An oxyacetylene torch
- A shrinker/stretcher
- A small metal brake

One last piece of advice: "If you're new to this, read as many articles and books as you can find on fabrication; videos are another good source of info," Bowers said.

1: Using chalk, lay out flames on 3- x 4-foot x ³/₁₆-inch flat steel. *Brenda Hoffman*

2: Using $1/4$-inch fine line tape, outline the flames; this gives you a $1/14$-inch-wide separation for the top and bottom dies. Then spray silver paint over flames. When it's dry, remove the tape to reveal precise inside and outside cut lines. *Brenda Hoffman*

3: Drill $3/8$-inch holes on each flame tip to facilitate saber saw cuts. *Brenda Hoffman*

4

5

4: The die pieces after ¹/₄ inch has been removed with the saber saw cuts. Note that the alignment marks are very critical when prepping to compress the dies onto the aluminum panel. *Brenda Hoffman*

5: Make the first cut inside of the flame design. The saber saw has a reciprocating action that works well on flat steel. *Brenda Hoffman*

6: Make the second cut on the outside edge of the flame die panel. *Brenda Hoffman*

7: Bevel the edges of the dies to allow the aluminum to slide when the dies are being compressed. *Brenda Hoffman*

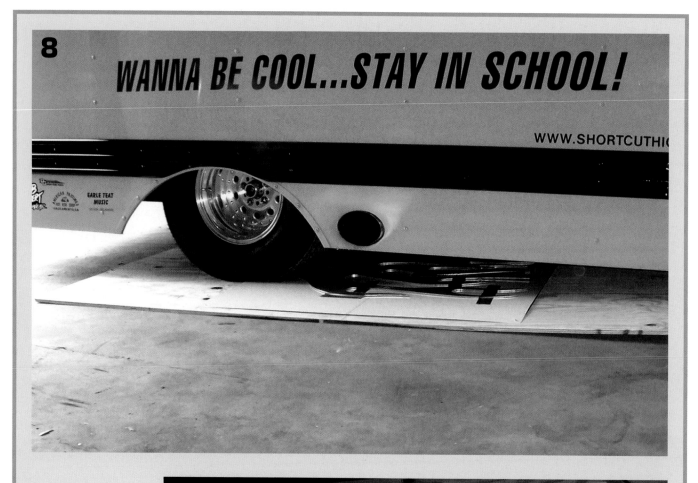

WANNA BE COOL...STAY IN SCHOOL!

WWW.SHORTCUTHI

8: Using the 6,000-pound weight of the bus, the flame design is pressed into the .023-gauge aluminum panel. *Brenda Hoffman*

9: The panel is now ready to be trimmed and fit into the inside car door panel. *Brenda Hoffman*

MEET THE PROS

Rick Dobbertin

"If a little is good ... and a lot is better ... then too much must be just right."

Like many an expert fabricator, Rick Dobbertin is an old-school, hands-on hot rodder—with a difference. The difference being in just what it is that he's laying his hands on these days: amphibious vehicles. How did a perfectly normal rodder go from building award-winning street machines to sailing a milk tank truck through the Panama Canal? "I had a speed shop where I specialized in superchargers, turbochargers, and nitrous injection," Dobbertin explains. "Then I got to thinking, why not stuff all of these systems into one car?"

"The 1965 Nova SS became my first radical project," he adds. "It was powered by a twin-turbocharged 454 Chevy and was *Hot Rod Magazine*'s Street Machine of the Year in 1982, and the winner of *Car Craft*'s 1982 and 1983 Street Machine Nationals. Bringing it to various shows I must have heard a hundred times, 'you've got two turbos, why only one blower?' So, I came up with the idea for the J-2000. I knew it would have to be more than that, so I listed every area that made a pro-streeter a pro-streeter." These included the following:

Rick Dobbertin is a fabricator with a taste for the unusual or outrageous.
Mary Dobbertin

This 1965 Nova was one of Dobbertin's first high-profile creations—a twin-turbocharged big-block-powered car that won accolades from *Hot Rod* and *Car Craft* magazines. *Mary Dobbertin*

- A massive engine with a radical induction system
- A racing transmission
- A narrowed rear axle
- Huge rear tires tucked way inside the body
- Narrow front tires, also tucked way in
- A full tubular frame and roll cage
- A very low stance, right on the ground
- Cool graphics and lots of colors
- Safety components, including a five-way harness, fire extinguisher, blower straps, and parachute

"I then decided to shoehorn all of that into the smallest, narrowest car that I could think of to exaggerate it even more," he says. "I ultimately chose the Pontiac J-2000."

When it was completed, the frame was made completely out of polished stainless steel. The engine was an all-aluminum small-block Chevy with aluminum heads. The induction system had two turbos, two superchargers, and nitrous oxide all coupled to a Lenco transmission—the only Lenco ever made out of aluminum instead of magnesium—and graphics by painter Chip Whittington.

Never one to miss an opportunity to go where none have gone before, Dobbertin took the J-2000 to Washington, D.C., for a photo shoot, burned some rubber in front of the Lincoln Memorial and popped the chute.

Rick Dobbertin got into cars because his father worked at General Motors for 34 years. His first wheeled invention was a bicycle that he converted into a hand-pedaled, rear-steer, "monster" when he was 10. He started building cars at age 11 with a Soap Box Derby racer, then progressed to go-karts and hot rods. And it was one of his rods, the J-2000 that, somewhat indirectly, led to his first amphibious vehicle, the Surface Orbiter.

"I went to Australia with the J-2000 for six weeks during their bicentennial, and we led the parade through Canberra," he says. "While I was there, I met a guy from Sweden and another from Germany who wanted me to bring the car to their countries, and I started thinking how cool it would be to build an amphibious car and drive it around the world."

For most people that would be the end of it—a cool idea perhaps, but that's not Dobbertin. Before long he was looking around trying to find just the right vehicle to modify for his Jules Verne adventure. What he found was a stainless-steel milk tanker. He reasoned that if it could keep 30,000 pounds of milk inside without leaking, it could keep the ocean out. He bought a used tanker for about $5,000, towed it home to his 39x13-foot garage, and started fabricating. Four and a half years and 14,000 man hours later, the tanker had morphed into the Surface

Rick's Pontiac J-2000 is outfitted with an aluminum small-block Chevy that breathes nitrous through the only twin-turbocharged, twin-supercharged induction system on the planet. *Mary Dobbertin*

Orbiter, a 32-foot-long, 8-foot-wide amphibious vehicle the likes of which had never been seen before outside of Hollywood.

Although his plan to circumnavigate the world came up a bit short due to lack of funding, he did manage to cover 30,000 miles on land and 3,000 miles of open water, visiting 38 states and 28 countries. Before the Orbiter became the first amphibian to sail/drive through the Panama Canal, Dobbertin took it across the open ocean to South America, where it received a mixed reception in a number of countries. One local in the Bahamas thought Dobbertin was from

outer space.

After all the touring around in the Orbiter, Rick dreamed of building another amphibious vehicle, one that would be the world's fastest amphibious craft: the HydroCar.

"People were always asking me how fast the Orbiter would go in the water. I'd say, 'Ten miles per hour,' and that would be the end of the conversation," Dobbertin says. "So, I decided to build something that would go 50 or 60 miles per hour on the water—the HydroCar.

"One of the best things about starting from scratch on a project car is you get to design and build every part that goes

One of Dobbertin's creations at speed in front of the Lincoln Memorial. *Mary Dobbertin*

into it. One of the worst things about starting from scratch on a project car is you have to design and build every part that goes into it.

"I've spent more time on designing and fabricating hinges and latches for the hood, door, and rear hatches than it will take to set up the entire drivetrain. Don't even get me started on the roof drip and windshield recess channels. These are parts that make it difficult to get motivated in the mornings."

Like other fabricators, Dobbertin uses cardboard, duct tape, and masking tape to model the parts for proper fit and overall looks before committing to cutting metal. Not surprisingly, the Hydro-Car presented many problems not encountered when building nonamphibious vehicles.

"Amphibians have an entire set of problems that conventional cars are not faced with," he explains. "The number one problem is they have to float—and they need to have their weight distributed in the right places so they don't lean to one side or front to back. They also have an entire set of problems that conventional boats are not faced with. They have to drive down the road, so they can't be too heavy, long, or wide to do that."

Two or three other amphibians have come out that can go 30 or 40 miles per hour on the water since Dobbertin began working on the HydroCar, so he changed his original design from using the 350 engine to the 670-horsepower 572 Chevy. Also, the wheelwells, which were going to be open to the water, will now be completely enclosed inside the sponsons with pneumatically actuated doors like aircraft have, so when the tires go up the entire bottom will be sealed off. The HydroCar will be the world's first tunnel-hull hydrofoil amphibian.

"I've done 99 percent of the designing and 100 percent of the welding on the car. I've had people help me form the big sheets of aluminum, which I then trim down and weld. The remaining work—the engine, transmission, axles, and marine drive—all that stuff will be a lot quicker than what's been done so far. Dick Clarke's Colors and Customs will handle the paint. I'll do some road tests with the sponsons off to make sure

This wild creation is the Surface Orbiter, an amphibious vehicle designed by Dobbertin to be driven around the world. *Rick and Mary Dobbertin*

everything is working properly, then attach the sponsons and put it in the water. It should be done and tested this year and out in public in the spring of 2006."

Like most hot rodders, Dobbertin is basically a seat-of-the-pants designer and builder. He did make detailed drawings before laying out the HydroCar frame, primarily because while the sponsons had to be as wide as possible to permit the tires to steer inside them, as well as to aid in flotation, the body still had to be as narrow as possible. A bulge was built into the middle section to accommodate the driver and passenger.

"The frame took a few months," he says. "It was essential that it be pretty much perfectly square because everything hangs off of the frame; so if it's off by a fourth of an inch here, a fourth of an inch inch there, it'll surely come back

Counting all the components and the through-frame tubes (to seal the assembly hardware from the seawater), the Orbiter's frame consisted of more than 900 parts—all welded, ground, and grained to make the frame look like a single piece of stainless steel. Dobbertin has always enjoyed building radical, one-of-a-kind projects. Heck, his initials are RAD. *Rick and Mary Dobbertin*

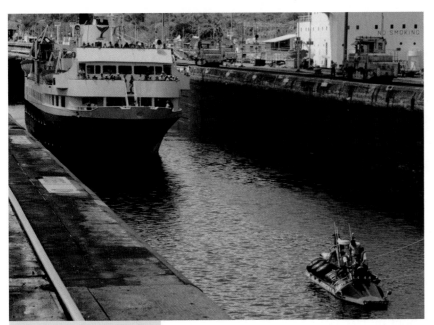

The Surface Orbiter in the Panama Canal. *Rick and Mary Dobbertin*

until the part you're working on is finished," he adds. "If you've got something that's a little bit crooked, don't think, 'I'll straighten it out with the next piece'—well it probably won't happen, and it will compound itself all the way down the line.

"There are a few things that make a big difference in the finished product that only take a few extra minutes and don't cost a dime. I always take the time to round the corners of every bracket I make; it makes them look more finished. I evenly space a series of bolts or rivets, then index the heads [or turn the bolt heads in the same direction] of all the hardware at the time of assembly. Also, always smooth out any caulk, and use it sparingly. If hanging a door or other body panels, try to keep the gaps to a minimum. Remember, those parts will be around for years to come."

Another thing he says is essential is setting up your workbench well. "Get one sturdier and bigger than you'll ever think that you'll need," Dobbertin says. "You'll need it. I also like having a narrow, movable workbench. This is great for working on two big projects at once, or moving it away from the stationary one to help hold a big section of a project."

When contemplating what he likes best about being a fabricator, Dobbertin says it shares some of the same creative characteristics as writing, painting, or designing buildings. "It takes some sort of compulsive behavior," he adds. "Anybody who spends this much time in the garage can't be completely right. People think it's the coolest thing to work on a car all day, but it's just like laying bricks or painting a house—it's labor. I seldom get up in the morning and think, 'Gosh it's seven o'clock, now I get to go out to the garage and work on the car all day.' While it's not always fun, it is rewarding."

"I sometimes look at the people that can afford to just go out and buy a finished car and think to myself, that would be the way to go, but then I stand back and look at something that I created with my own two hands and, I have to say, the feeling that comes over me is something that you just can't buy—although I would like to try it just once."

to bite you later. The HydroCar is within one-sixteenth inch from right to left.

"Another thing that people don't realize is that when you build an amphibian, you can't just drill a hole through the frame for a bolt. You have to weld a tube in the frame, or it's going to fill the frame up with water. You also can't torque those bolts without the tubes because you'll just squeeze the frame together."

The HydroCar's center frame section is stainless steel and all of the sponson parts—frames and skins—are aluminum. Everything was ultimately bonded together with a marine-grade caulk, which, according to Dobbertin, is "a real bear." "I had no way to form the body panels, so I ended up having to cut and TIG weld almost every corner," he says. "It was an arduous task—welded inside and out—I used templates for everything. A real time saver was the special chop saw blade for cutting the aluminum that I bought."

Dobbertin used the main stainless-steel frame as the jig for the sponsons. "It essentially became the welding table for them during the fabrication process," he says.

"I foam-filled the sponsons with marine-grade flotation foam, then ground it all down, and painted it with white enamel paint."

"If you don't catch your mistakes someone else will, so you should never move on to the next part of something

MEET THE PROS

Mark Carpenter

"I love to have people say, 'You made that yourself?'"

Mark Carpenter, president of MTJ Manufacturing Inc. and MTJ Truck Equipment Inc., is a master metal fabricator—a certified welder whose work encompasses everything from custom toolboxes and pool parts to giant truck bodies, fences, shipping containers, wrestling rings, and the odd shrimp boat. His background is typical in that he learned by watching, listening, and practicing, until he got it right.

"Books and videos are a great way to learn, but nothing beats practice," Carpenter says. "You can go to a trade school and take some classes, or try and find someone who can show you what to do. When I was 17, I had a mentor who was a U.S. Navy diver and underwater welder. A mentor is really the way, someone to push you along—try this, try that, looks good, keep it up."

Carpenter's early training came in high school, when he took three years of auto shop. The culmination of his classes came his senior year, when he placed second in the Plymouth Trouble Shooting Contest statewide competition. "A friend of mine had a car that we were putting an engine in and had to weld in a motor mount. When I tried to weld it, some of our classmates started laughing at me, and I said to myself, 'No, that is not going to happen again' and off I went and here I am today," he says.

His fabrication business was a side job for years, something he'd work in after putting in time as a heavy-duty truck and industrial equipment mechanic. "Eventually, I bought a truck body shop from a gentleman who was retiring, and it was tough at first," Carpenter says. "I was a young guy with no real experience running a business like that with a fast-growing amount of overhead. I kept purchasing various pieces of equipment to expand the business. In the late 1980s, I almost lost everything, but I restructured and came back by doing everything right—being straightforward—if it can't be done, be truthful, and don't lie about it."

If there is one aspect of Carpenter's work that makes it stand out from the crowd, it is his custom wrestling rings.

"I got into that through a friend of mine," he says. "The WWE [World Wrestling Entertainment] had bought some scissor lifts that needed to be modified and the supplier could not make the modifications. They wanted to use them sort of like Roman chariots to run the gladiators/wrestlers to and from the ring. So we took the lifts and installed stops to allow a maximum height above the floor of about eight feet to the platform, and

Mark Carpenter on the steps of the portable two-piece stairs for a wrestling ring.

we put posts and ropes to make them look like mini-rings. We installed a rear driver's seat with pedals and a steering wheel–operated cable over a hydraulic power steering system like those found on large boats, and then added an electric hydraulic high-volume pump to give it a faster speed. When the wrestlers would get into the platform area, they would raise the platform so as to be able to be seen anywhere from the floor of the arena, and off they went in their chariots."

Now, Carpenter has built between 50 or 55 custom rings, many in different sizes. One was even designed so that it could be disassembled and put into a freight elevator to be moved up to a fourth-floor restaurant. The rings weigh about 4,800 pounds, with the corner posts alone weighing in at about 200 pounds. "We've built so many that we have a jig for every part now," Carpenter says.

The more typical MTJ project, though, is a specialized custom truck body, which can be used in a variety of applications.

The lumber truck MTJ built features a hydraulically operated tilting-slider body with rollers embedded in the bed to facilitate unloading lumber. The body also has multiple tie-down strapping anchors and can be used to lock off different sections of the load to allow multiple deliveries without moving the entire load.

"The truck took about three months [while working on other projects] from start to finish, which included drawing up the all-new design," Carpenter says. "In custom work you have to fabricate just about everything; everything has to be made specifically for that particular truck and checked and double-checked before it leaves here. People don't realize the amount of time it takes to fabricate things. Some items—like hinges, locks, hydraulic cylinders, and valves—can be purchased for less than we can make them in house. As for the other items, it's not like you can buy them off the shelf— you have to cut everything, fit everything, put it all together, make sure it's square, make sure the customer is getting what they wanted and, most important, what they are paying for. If you don't follow it through with good construction ethics, nothing will be worth a damn. Quality takes time."

The specially designed aluminum striping truck cab was built to replace one that had been damaged beyond repair in a crash.

"We did all the window cutouts first on a bench, then attached the panels to the frame, built the top, sliding rear door, went to paint, soundproofing, then installed it on the truck," Carpenter says.

As for the aforementioned "odd shrimp boat," it is a good example of what a custom fabrication shop can be called upon to build. The boat, a 70-footer, had been partially destroyed in a fire that completely burned off the wheelhouse and crew quarters. The project of assisting in designing and building the crew quarters and wheelhouse was brought to Carpenter after a local shipyard turned down the work for being too small of a project to be bothered with.

"My son and I measured everything, set datum points, made up the drawings, had the drawings approved, ordered the materials, and went to work," Carpenter says. "The wheelhouse is my design. I made up some concept drawings on the computer, laid it out on the floor of the shop with templates, and fabricated it entirely out of aluminum; the same with the crew quarters. They were then shipped to the marina where the pieces were fitted together, welded, and attached to the hull with key lock–type construction, stainless-steel fasteners, and epoxy."

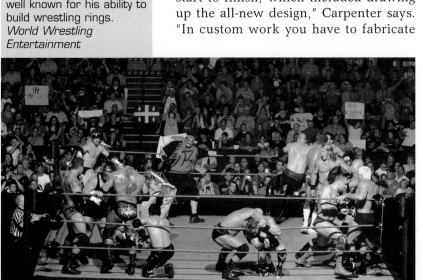

One of Carpenter's less portable works. He never intended to become so well known for his ability to build wrestling rings. *World Wrestling Entertainment*

MEET THE PROS

Jerry Bowers

"This thing definitely is a square peg, 'cause it sure doesn't fit into any round holes."

Hot rodders are by nature different from the rest of us when it comes to eyeballing a vehicle. To a hot rodder, every old car or truck is a potential project, something to be chopped, slammed, bagged, tagged, and driven downtown on cruise nights. Yet Jerry Bowers let his hot rodder tendencies go over the edge a bit, if you will, when he decided that his next hot rod would come from a school bus.

Growing up on a small farm in rural Virginia, Bowers first developed his hot rodding interest at an early age, taking things apart and putting them back together again—not always in their original form.

"We were basically poor farm folks and there wasn't much money for store-bought toys and such, so we made our own," Bowers says. "I started by customizing toy cars, and by the time I was in high school I'd moved up to a '37 Chevy coupe. I was about 16, had no equipment, no knowledge, no nothing, but my brothers and I messed around with it a bit."

He took some industrial arts classes in high school, but when he graduated he got a job in a sign shop and worked in that business for 25 years. Yet he always had a car project going on at home—building a T-bucket roadster with a 318 Plymouth motor, a '53 Merc that was slammed and panel scalloped, a couple of Plymouth ex-cop cars, and a slammed '69 Charger with lake pipes, racing discs, shaved door handles, and frenched lights.

While attending a car show in Maryland in the late 1980s, Bowers first thought about a hot rod project that no one else had yet attempted: building a hot rod school bus.

"I was talking to some other rodders and the subject of school buses came up and why no one had chopped or lowered one, and I thought, yeah, a five-foot-tall school bus—cool," he says.

"I'd done some work for a guy who had an old 1949 Ford F-5 bus, and we worked out a barter deal for lettering his truck, which is the way it is when you're operating on a shoestring. He towed it over and parked it in front of my shop. It was atrocious."

The bus was built in 27-inch segments, so Bowers and his friends care-

Jerry Bowers with a work in progress. *Jerry Bowers*

Left: Bowers customized this hot rod pickup, which uses a 1947 Ford four-door sedan front clip mated to a truck rear. He fabricated a Carson-style lift-off top for the hot rod. *Jerry Bowers*

Right: This hot rod school bus is another Bowers creation. *Jerry Bowers*

fully disassembled the sections, then pushed the rear end forward and folded it back together. "Then we started chopping," Bowers says.

His original plan was to fabricate a rectangular tube frame and install a new Ford motor in it, but a friend who owned a salvage yard suggested using the frame of a Cadillac Eldorado instead. It was the perfect solution as the frame was flat, and with front-wheel-drive there would be no driveshaft hump in the floor. When the frame arrived, the body was jacked up, the old frame pulled out, the new one moved into place, and the shortened body lowered onto it. Although it would take some major modifications to make the frame suitable for the heavy bus body, the first major step had been taken. Now the real work could begin, five years of it.

"The top sheet metal wasn't in too bad a shape, but it had coats and coats of paint on it," Bowers explains. "We decided that instead of trying to get it all off, we'd replace most of the sheet metal in the boxed area with .040-gauge aluminum. It ended up with about 80 percent being aluminum, with the front and rear made of steel. The front fenders were widened three inches, raised two inches, and two inches were trimmed off of the bottom of the hood. Everything was MIG welded into a single-section tilt front end. We also designed and built a driver's-side door with an electric window."

Bowers decided, though, that he really wanted to retain the bus' floppy doors and keep them hand operated and at the same proportions they were in the original vehicle. "By the time I was done, it took about eight different cuts to end up with the windows and everything in proportion," he says. "Once it was welded, I sent it off to a friend in Michigan who does bodywork, and he finished them off. My brother Wayne did the upholstery. He took some plywood and foam, carved it out, and it's as plush as can be. We kept the original dashboard, glove box, and instrument panel, and added a Pontiac tilt steering column."

The bus, now christened Shortcut High, is almost constantly on tour, visiting schools throughout the country where Jerry and his partner, Brenda, try to impress on students the importance of the bus' motto: Wanna Be Cool, Stay in School. With the program having recently achieved nonprofit status, Bowers is now working on plans to fabricate some new buses in order to get the message out to even more kids.

"I want to give a special thanks to my girlfriend, Brenda, and my brother Dennis," he says. "Without their tireless dedication to the project, Shortcut High could never have happened."

Another project near and dear to Jerry's hot-rodder heart is his 1947 Ford four-door sedan–based pickup truck. Built with Ramsey Mosher of Rams Rod Shop (builder of Terry Cook's '39 Lincoln Scrape), it was one of the first cars to be turned into a pickup.

"Most people make them out of two-door coupes or convertibles," Bowers says. "I didn't want a two-door body because the doors are too long. To me, they look all out of proportion."

WELDING

If you're going to work with metal, you need to know how to weld. It's not hard, but you need to practice. A lot. Anyone can do it, though. Here's how.

Welding is one of the essential skills to crafting your own personal monster.

"Welding technique is essential."
— Rick Dobbertin, aquatic car builder

Some welding techniques have been around for more than 80 years and are still being used in today's top welding shops, but those early methods—oxyacetylene gas welding and heliarc welding—have now largely been supplanted by two newer processes: metal inert gas (MIG) welding and tungsten inert gas (TIG) welding. In fact, every one of the fabricators included in this book recommended the MIG welder as an essential item for anyone setting up a metal fabrication shop.

"If you're just starting out, I'd recommend a 110 machine, a MIG, or wire-fed machine, which is the easiest process to learn," welder Lisa Legohn says. "It's fast—you can learn to do a competent weld in about a week. Get yourself a good basic instruction book and practice, practice, practice."

Space

A good welding environment requires proper lighting, good ventilation without excessive drafts or extreme cold, and a sturdy metal workbench set at the height most comfortable for working.

Equipment

As noted, the MIG welder is the first choice for a new shop setup, but as there are a number of different types of MIG units, it will be up to you to choose the one that best fits your purposes.

MIG welders come in different rated amperages, generally between 60 and 160 amps. The higher the amperage, the thicker the metal you can weld. A 100-amp or better unit is good for welding up to $1/4$-inch steel.

The MIG works by continuously feeding a thin wire into the weld puddle via an electric motor-drive system, along with an argon gas shield to keep the

Choose the welder that best fits your purposes.

metal from oxidizing. To operate it, you need only turn on the power, turn on the gas, point the trigger, and weld.

You can also get a "gasless" MIG unit fitted with a flux core wire, which produces the same effect as argon gas, but without the gas bottle. This unit is more portable than the standard MIG.

Depending on the skill of the operator, a MIG machine can weld up to 24 inches of .050 steel per minute, which is nearly four times as fast as the other modern unit, the TIG welder.

"Probably the biggest mistake made when using a MIG is to pull the gun while welding instead of pushing it," Eddie Paul says, "which keeps the gas in front of the weld and produces a much better result."

A TIG welder produces a very high-

Safety gloves are a must when welding or using a cutting torch or plasma cutter.

temperature, very confined arc that heats metal to the melting point for the purpose of fusion welding, yet uses less heat than either MIG or gas welding units. It offers the welder the most control of any welding process and accomplishes fusion without the addition of filler rod, eliminating extra weld seam buildup. Once the arc is struck and a molten weld puddle started, it can be maintained with the unit's amp controls for as long as needed. This means that there is always enough time to properly add filler rod material to the puddle.

"The TIG makes a nice, even weld, but you have to watch the metals melting," Mark Carpenter says. "You have to know when to fuse it. When you do aluminum, you have to look for the puddle and watch it

The plasma cutter is the jack-of-all trades of metal working.

A good helmet is another important accessory when welding. Modern models have light-sensing shields that darken when you strike the arc.

Welding is so easy, even a robot can do it.

TIG (tungsten inert gas) welding equipment is very expensive for home use, but provides the ultimate in control.

flow together; a lot of people when they're first starting put the wire in, lay it down, and are done with it. You have to lay the wire in place and melt it to see what's going on. You have to see the joint; if you can't, there's no sense welding the job. If you put too small an amount of heat to it, you won't weld anything, and if you over throttle the control pedal, you'll go right through the material.

"The only way to learn how to do it right is to practice, practice, practice. It doesn't come for free—it takes time. Some people complain that the TIG is hard to work with; well, anything's hard to work with if you don't know how to use it."

Over the years, the oldest welding process, oxyacetylene welding, has remained based upon oxygen and acetylene gas mixing, igniting, and producing a high-temperature flame. This type of unit is primarily used today for cutting torches, but they are still reliable for welding jobs that don't require pinpoint application, as the area heated by the torch is much broader than with either MIG or TIG units.

The welder you select will probably be the single most important initial acquisition for your new shop. Although a name-brand welder may cost a few dollars more, most fabricators agree these pieces of equipment are worth it. They are generally better built by manufacturers who stand behind their products with warranties and readily available parts in most areas or via the Internet. But buying a name-brand welder does not mean you have to purchase new equipment. Tent sales are often a great place to find bargains on name-brand equipment. The Internet is also a viable option, the major drawback being that you can't actually see the unit before you purchase it, which can cause obvious headaches.

The most important, and necessary, accessory to your new welding rig is a welding helmet. This is not an item to try and save a few dollars on. The latest technology may cost more, but no one wants to put a price on his or her eyesight. Eye burns from the UV rays present in arc welding can cause cataracts or even eye cancer. The newest welding helmets feature an electronic face shield lens that changes density almost instantaneously as soon as an arc is struck, becoming three or four times darker. In addition to reducing eyestrain, they also contribute to much more accurate arc starts than the older style helmets, which required the torch to be aimed at the weld joint with the helmet shield up, then started once the shield was lowered.

Welding is hot, grimy, and, without the proper precautions, dangerous. And according to Eric Scarlett, who helped build a Porsche golf collector, "You're going to get burned."

A NASCAR team member TIG welds a tubular suspension member using a Lincoln Precision TIG 275 welder. Note the clean, tidy, and well-lit welding area, which contributes greatly to making good, sound welds. *Lincoln Electric Company*

The only company that can legally call its TIG welders "Heliarc" is ESAB Welding & Cutting Products of Florence, South Carolina. In this illustration, you can see the schematic of a TIG welding setup. *ESAB Welding & Cutting Products*

In order to melt metal for fusion you need a lot of heat, at least 2,700 degrees Fahrenheit for welding steel. But you can take certain preventive actions to lessen the number of times you singe yourself. These include wearing leather sleeves and gloves and doing whatever it takes to remind yourself not to touch a just-welded joint with your bare skin. You should also always cover all exposed skin when welding as the UV rays can also cause melanoma, or skin cancer, and you must also make sure that anyone else in close proximity to the welding process is aware of its potential dangers.

Comparing Welding Processes: TIG, MIG and Oxyacetylene

The first welding process used in building airplanes was oxyacetylene gas. In the early 1930s, many airplanes were assembled by gas welding mild-steel tubing together to form an airplane's structure.

A reprint of a 1932 airplane builders' handbook specifies gas welding SAE 1025 thin-wall steel tubing to build airplane fuselages. Most mild-steel tubing specified for building airplanes was 3/4-inch and 1/2-inch diameter by 0.035-inch wall thickness. Chrome-moly 4130 steel tubing did not become generally available to amateur builders until several years after World War II.

Heliarc welding came next, generally in the mid- to late 1950s. But Heliarc welding equipment was relatively expensive and very bulky at first.

Wire-feed welding, now called MIG welding, first became popular for heavy-duty welding in the auto industry, where manufacturers used this process to mass produce car and truck frames. This chapter will explain the processes to help you decide which best suits your finances and your intended projects.

TIG Welding

In TIG welding, a very high-temperature, but very confined, arc is formed that heats the base metal to the melting point for the purpose of fusion welding.

TIG welding uses less heat to join metal than either MIG or gas welding. TIG welding is by far the most controllable of all manual (not automatic) welding processes. It is so accurate that you could weld a thin piece of 0.010-inch steel sheet to a thick piece of 6.000-inch steel billet and not burn through the thin sheet, yet get good penetration into the thick billet.

In fact, TIG welding allows for fusion welding without the addition of filler rod, making it possible to produce welds without extra weld seam buildup. And with a foot-pedal amp control or a thumb amp control on the TIG torch, you can actually strike an arc, start a tiny weld puddle and without moving the puddle or adding welding rod, you can maintain the same weld molten puddle for minutes or even hours at a time. That is how controllable TIG welding is.

The advantage to having such precise puddle control is that it provides adequate time to properly add filler rod material to the puddle. You can strike an arc, form a puddle, then you can carefully and accurately add just the right amount of filler rod at exactly the right place in the molten weld puddle.

MIG Welding

Commonly called wire-feed welding because a thin wire is fed into the weld puddle by an electric motor-drive system, this emerging process is quickly gaining in popularity because it is easy to operate and relatively fast. A TIG welder can weld about 6 inches of 0.050-inch steel sheet in one minute, whereas a MIG welder can weld up to 24 inches of the same material in one minute.

There are pros and cons to MIG welding the more exotic thin-wall 4130 steel tubes and thin sheets of 4130 steel used in aircraft construction. Here are some of the considerations:

Pros of MIG Welding

It is easy to turn the power switch on, turn the gas on, and merely point the gun and pull the trigger to wire-feed weld race car frames and aircraft fuselage structures. It is possible to weld a lot more inches of weld bead per hour with MIG welding than with any other welding process. The reason is that the welding filler metal is continuously fed from a spool of wire into the weld for as long as the welder holds the welding gun trigger.

A MIG weld bead is usually a very sound weld, almost as sound as a perfectly done TIG weld. Once the amps, volts, and wire-feed speed are properly adjusted, MIG welding is a very high-quality welding process.

Cons of MIG Welding

Several problems associated with MIG welding include the normal tendency of an electrode-fed arc weld to start off cold. This means that each start of the

Typical MIG or wire-feed welding setups require these basic elements for operation. *Lincoln Electric Company*

Figure 245.—A Typical Portable Welding Outfit, Employing Both Welding Gases (Oxygen and Acetylene) in Safety Storage Cylinders, Mounted on a Two-Wheeled Truck. This Outfit Weighs Less Than 300 Lbs., and May Be Handled Easily by One Man.

Gas welding setups have not changed much since the early years. This drawing shows a typical commercial oxyacetylene welding rig used in the 1930s. *Author's collection*

MIG welding with a 75 percent/25 percent CO2 /argon gas outer shield is the fastest, but least accurate, of all manual welding processes. *Gayle Finch*

Gas welding (oxyacetylene gas), is a relatively clean and dependable metal joining process, although it is less accurate than TIG welding. However, gas welding is far less expensive than most other welding processes. *Gayle Finch*

wire can slip into the crack and fail to make a weld bead. Another disadvantage of welding small-diameter thin-wall tubing with MIG is that once you accidentally burn a hole in the tubing, it is very hard to fill the hole without stopping to make a patch for it. There may also be times you will have to use gas welding to patch holes made by MIG welding.

The primary difficulty with MIG welding is that once you squeeze the trigger on the MIG gun, you are committed to move along with making a weld bead, ready or not. If you make a bad start, sometimes you have to stop, grind, or cut out the bead weld, and then start over again.

arc is not fully penetrated for the first fractions of an inch of weld bead. Once the MIG weld bead is established, the heat and penetration is normal, but it always starts off cold.

Another disadvantage to MIG welding is that the process is highly intolerant of any gaps in the fit-up of the parts. MIG wire is usually 0.025 inch to 0.030 inch in diameter, and if there is a gap larger than the diameter of the electrode, the

Gas Welding

The oldest aircraft welding process is still good and dependable. Oxyacetylene welding is very much the same as it was in 1920. The two gases, oxygen and the fuel gas acetylene, are still the same as they have been for 100 years or more. Gas welding torches have slowly evolved over the years, but a torch made 50 years ago would still be a dependable aircraft welding torch. And gas welding rigs are still the least expensive of all welding setups.

The neutral flame combines an equal

pressure of oxygen and acetylene to produce a flame temperature at the inner core of about 5,000 degrees Fahrenheit, a temperature that is also used in TIG welding. The difference is that the oxyacetylene flame produces fewer Btus (British thermal units, a measurement of heat units) and much more lower-temperature heat at its outer flame.

In the process of welding a butt joint of thin-wall tubing, the heat-affected area of the tube will be several times larger with gas welding than with TIG or MIG welding. But this is seldom a problem. The gas welding flame does heat the assembly more, but in steel and aluminum with thicknesses of less than 0.100 inch, the gas welding torch is very adequate.

There are a few difficulties with gas welding. When you are attempting to weld inside corners, the flame is blown back toward you, and that makes the heat on your hands uncomfortable. Another difficulty is welding next to an edge of tubing or plate. The heat of the torch is considerably broader than with TIG or MIG welding, and this causes sharp edges to want to melt away. The solution is to add extra length to the metal joint to be welded and then trim it to the correct size after completing the weld.

Welding Equipment

Here's a rundown on today's welding equipment choices.

Square-Wave Technology

Welding equipment technology has advanced significantly, and square-wave technology is now available to provide a very smooth output-welding arc in AC aluminum- and magnesium-welding modes. Square-wave technology also smoothes out the DC welding output when welding steel, stainless steel, and titanium. Take my advice, and do not buy a new TIG or MIG welding machine until you have compared square-wave

Left: The dream of many home shop welders—and a great portable weld rig as well— is this thermodynamics 190-amp TIG welder that runs off 110-volt 220-volt shop current. It's a DC-only welder that sells for about $1,500, but it only weighs 19 pounds!

Right: Tim Marr of Lincoln Electric Company proudly shows a top-of-the-line Lincoln square-wave 355-amp TIG and stick welder that has numerous extra features. This machine sells for $3,600 without cart, cooler, and argon cylinders, making the cost for a complete unit about $4,500.

A NASCAR Valvoline race car team member is using the Lincoln Invertec V205-T TIG welder to add a mounting tab to an aluminum racing radiator. The V205-T welder sells for under $3,000. Look for special lower price sales on this welder at air and car shows, as well as racing events. *Lincoln Electric Company*

technology with earlier AC/DC equipment. My guess is that you'll choose one of the square-wave welders, which are now manufactured by all name-brand welder companies.

Portable Rigs

Trailer- or truck-mounted portable welding rigs are rapidly becoming a thing of the past. New inverter technology makes it possible to carry a pipe-welding-capacity power supply not much larger than your arc-welding helmet in the trunk of your car. At this time, however, inverter welders will not weld aluminum or magnesium, but that should change soon.

Modular Add-Ons

For about half the price of the lowest-cost TIG welder, you can purchase a modular TIG add-on that features capacitor start or, in some products, high-frequency (the best) start. This means that if you have a good old stick welder or a good old wire-feed welder, you can use its transformer to power a TIG torch, even with a foot-pedal control and argon-gas timing.

Electronic Welding Helmets

For many years, welders who did stick, TIG, and MIG welding were forced to aim the torch, stick, or gun at the weld with their helmets up, then shake their head to lower their helmet, and hope their aim at the weld joint had not moved. This problem was the biggest obstacle to learning to weld quickly.

One of the best labor-saving inventions to come along in many years is this plasma cutting machine that can cut steel, aluminum, copper, stainless steel, or any metal that will conduct electricity. This Lincoln Electric Company Pro-Cut 55 only weighs 55 pounds. It sells for under $2,700 and can be purchased at welding supply outlets as well as at car shows, air shows, and special welding events. This particular machine works off 220 volts of AC current. *Lincoln Electric Company*

Even us old-timers never really mastered the flip-the-helmet-down trick. We always had to stop welding, raise the helmet, and look to see if we had made a good weld.

Very recently, some savvy engineer designed an electronic welding lens that is a shade 3 (sunglasses shade) when no welding arc is present. The lens shade changes to a 10, 11, or 12 as soon as an arc is struck, but the change is not instantaneous. You do see the arc, but only for about 1/500th to 1/125,000th of a second. What this means is that at the end of a long day of arc welding, your eyes will itch about as much as if you

had spent the day at the beach without sunglasses. These helmets run from $100 to $275, or more. They really do contribute to much more accurate arc starts in stick, TIG, and MIG welding, as well as plasma arc cutting.

Thumb Controls

You will not always be able to TIG weld at tabletop level. Some welds must be reached by standing on a ladder or by crouching 6 inches off the floor. For many years, the solution to these hard-to-reach TIG welds was to lay a brick on the foot pedal and hope for the right amount of heat from the torch or to go

Left: The real Heliarc welders, made by ESAB Welding & Cutting Products of Florence, South Carolina. These 252-amp and 352-amp TIG and stick welders also feature square-wave technology. *ESAB Welding & Cutting Products*

Right: Modular TIG adapters, such as this MTA160 sold by Daytona MIG, make it possible to use the transformer from a MIG welder or a DC-only stick welder and have TIG capabilities at a cost of less than $1,000, including torch and foot pedal.

Left: Electronic welding helmets let the welder see the TIG, MIG, or stick at a No. 3 shade (sunglasses) before striking the arc, then change to a 10, 11, or 12 lens shade within 1/100,000th of a second after the arc is started. Cost: $100 to $350.

Right: The back side of the Jackson electronic welding helmet shows the five buttons that adjust the helmet's operating shades.

This water-cooled TIG torch is being run by a Lincoln Electric Company Square Wave TIG 175 welder. The TIG torch is a "speedway" model that is made by the TEC torch company. For delicate TIG welding projects on steel, stainless steel, aluminum, and titanium, this torch is one that is preferred by many welders. The torch is cooled by a simple water bucket and swamp cooler pump when it is welding thick materials. *Gayle Finch*

Tim Marr demonstrates the TIG torch thumb control that starts and stops this large water-cooled torch without the need for a foot control. You cannot operate a TIG foot control when you are on your knees trying to weld something afoot off the floor.

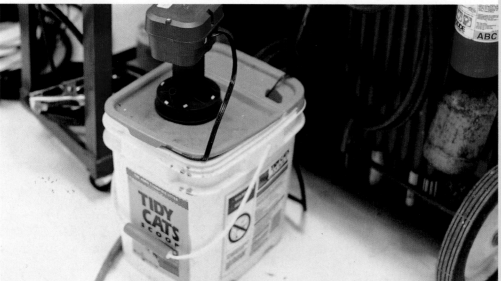

Top Left: An often-forgotten accessory for a TIG welder is a second argon flowmeter for back-gas purging stainless-steel and titanium welds.

Top Right: Every TIG welder needs to ask Santa Claus to bring him one of these TIG Cradles made by the Ratermann Manufacturing Company of Santa Clara, California. It conveniently holds all the TIG parts a welder needs.

Middle: This heavy-duty TIG- or MIG-torch water pump pays for itself by recirculating cooling water rather than wasting the water down the drain.

Bottom: In a pinch, you can make your own TIG torch water cooling tank, as shown here. You will need a five-gallon plastic bucket with a lid, two bricks (which should be placed in the bottom of the bucket), and an evaporative air conditioner water pump. To set this tank up, just connect the outlet of the pump to the inlet hose on the torch and put the outlet hose of the torch back into the bucket. For long-term use, you should use a 25/75 mixture of automotive antifreeze and clean water. The water becomes stagnant unless you add antifreeze.
Gayle Finch

find a helper to push the pedal for you. Welds made this way were never as good as they could have been.

The solution to this TIG welding problem is to buy a thumb- or finger-operated TIG amp control switch and attach it to your TIG torch. You won't use the thumb- or finger-control TIG switch much, but when you need it, you'll be happy you have it.

Consumables

Products used up in the course of welding are called consumables. They include welding and brazing rod, wire on spools, flux for brazing, solder and pastes for soldering, and even MIG gun parts, plasma-cutter parts, TIG cups, and tungsten.

Fitting and Cleaning

A properly fitted and cleaned weld assembly makes the welding process much easier and more sound than a poorly fitted, dirty assembly. Fitting is the most time-consuming part of welding any assembly, but fitting is also the major contributor to good high-quality welds.

Several years ago, while working as a

nuclear power plant welding inspector, I noticed that the pipe fitters did about 80 percent of the work, and the higher-paid welders did only 20 percent of the work in fabricating the piping in the nuclear power plant. You will find the same time ratio in fitting and welding aircraft or race car assemblies.

File to Fit

Numerous books on pipe and tube welding offer many solutions to fish-mouthing tubing. Some welders actually dress several widths of abrasive grinding wheels to a half-circle, and grind the fish-mouth into each tube end! Others try to band-saw the fishmouth into the tube, then finish the notch with a half-round file. Still others mount a milling cutter in a lathe and push the tube into the cutter, which can be rather dangerous.

Hole Saw

Then some clever fabricator designed a hole saw mandrel and an adjustable tubing clamp assembly and revolutionized the fitting of tubing for welding. In the photos in this chapter, you can see how easy it is to cut tubing to the exact angle and the exact fishmouth size. The entire process to set up for a 52-degree angle cut in a piece of $^{11}/_{12}$-inch x 0.95-inch wall thickness tube is about one minute. The actual cut takes even less time.

After the hole saw fishmouth cut is made, remove the burrs around the saw cut with a file or a sanding belt. The area to be welded must then be sanded clean of mill scale and cleaned with acetone before the weld is made.

Left: Every welding project begins with cutting the materials into the proper lengths. A cut-off saw like the one being used here by Mitch Matthews costs about $200 and will save lots of hacksaw work.

Right: For nearly 75 years, filing fishmouth joints in tubular structures was the best way to ensure a good fit-up. Today, there is a better way to do this task.

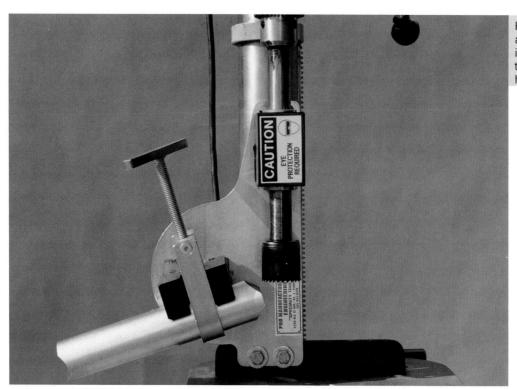

Hole saw fishmouth tools can accurately make tubular fit-ups in just a fraction of the time it takes to do the same job by hand. *Pro Tools*

Fitting the Parts Before Welding

The fit-up of tubing or parts to be welded is the most essential part of weld preparation. Do a good fit-up and your weld will be much easier to do, and it will be stronger and prettier! Here are some tips you should know:

Fit every part to have a gap that's less than the thickness of the welding rod being used. In most cases, the gap between aircraft parts to be welded should be less than 0.020 inch. If the welding rod can be inserted between the parts, the fit-up is less than ideal and is too loose for a good, strong weld.

Wide gaps can be filled, but bridging open air between the parts causes hot spots in the weld, and the air gap on the back side of the weld allows atmospheric contaminants such as hydrogen and oxygen to weaken and crack the weld. These wide gaps in the weld will cause fatigue cracking in the weld at a later time. Hidden hot cracking often occurs in poorly fitted joints.

Weld joints will last a lifetime if properly designed and fitted before welding. Take an extra 5 or 10 minutes and fit the joints properly.

Tubing joints can be fitted perfectly if you use one of the hole saw tubing notchers that are on the market. They sell for $149 to $279, and they can make fitting tubes much easier than filing and grinding each fishmouth by hand.

CAUTION:

When using a bi-metal hole saw to fishmouth steel tubing less than 1 inch in diameter and with less than 0.049-inch wall thickness, be aware of the fact that the coarse hole saw blade teeth can shatter if special care is not taken to cut very slowly. You must engage the saw into the tubing very slowly to avoid shattering all the teeth off the hole saw tube.

Quite likely, some enterprising manufacturer will see the opportunity to make a special bi-metal hole saw for cutting thin-wall tubing. Ideally, a $\frac{1}{2}$-inch diameter hole saw should have 15 teeth per inch rather than the 6 to 8 teeth per inch that is currently available. Meanwhile, cut small, thin tubes slowly.

Mount your Joint Jigger fish-mouth tool on your workbench and operate it with a $1/2$-inch drill motor. It will notch rectangular tubing.

Clean the Parts Thoroughly Before Welding

All new metal will have oil and scale on it—even 4130 steel, stainless steel, and aluminum will not be ready to weld as it comes to you from the supplier. Stainless steel will have oil or even protective paper and sticky glue on it. Aluminum will have oil or paper or aluminum oxide on it, and 4130 chrome-moly steel will have pickling oil and mill scale on it when it comes to you. This "dirt" will contaminate the weld if it is not removed prior to welding.

All old, used, repairable metal will have paint, oil, rust, corrosion, and oxidation on it. This dirt absolutely must be cleaned off before welding. Dirt contaminates and weakens welds.

Recommended Cleaning Methods Prior to Welding

Chrome-moly steel (4130) must be sanded to a bright, new-appearing metal under the gray mill scale on the surface of the tubing, 4130 steel sheet, or plate. The mill scale must be cleaned off 1 inch back from the edge to be welded. Tubing can be hand sanded with strip emery paper of about 80 grit, like shining your shoes. You can also use open screen–type sanding strips to clean the mill scale off the tubes. Flat sheets of 4130 steel can be sanded by hand, block sanding the edges back to 1 inch from the edge to be welded. Use a piece of 80- to 120-grit emery paper and wrap it around a block of wood to make the sanding easier.

CAUTION:

Do not, under any circumstances, sand thin-wall tubing or thin sheet metal with a power sanding belt or disc since power sanding would remove too much metal and severely weaken the metal in the welded zone. Hand sanding is the only safe way to remove mill scale and oxidation from metal to be welded.

Sandblasting or glass-bead cleaning will safely clean off mill scale and oxidation, but the cleanup process to remove all the sand or glass dust from the part is not worth the time it takes. You absolutely do not want to weld your valuable parts if they are covered with sand dust and glass dust.

Also, do not attempt to remove mill scale and oxidation with a power wire brush because the brush will imbed metal from its bristles into the metal to be welded, and this wire brush metal will contaminate your welds. Also, if the power wire brush is quite stiff, it will actually erode the parts to be welded and cause them to be weakened in the weld zone where you cleaned them.

Top: Every tube must be cleaned before welding. Here a strip of carborundum emery cloth is used to sand the thin film of mill scale off a $^3/_4$ x 0.032-inch chrome-moly tube. Every place that will be welded must be cleaned like this.

Bottom: After the mill scale is sanded off the tube, use a paper towel soaked with acetone to remove all traces of oil and dust before the tube is welded.

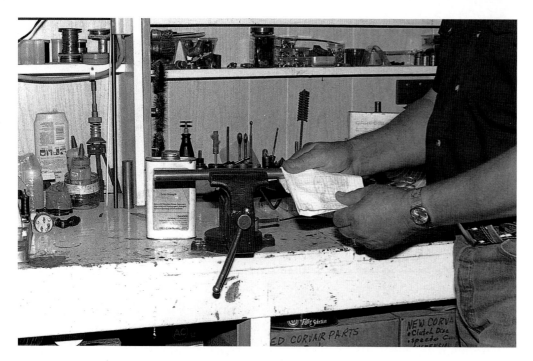

Just a few minutes prior to welding, clean the weld area of the tubes of sheet metal with acetone or denatured alcohol and a clean, white lint-free cloth to remove all grease and oil. Fingerprint oils contaminate welds, too. Clean the parts as thoroughly as if you were going to paint them. Do not expect the heat from welding to evaporate the dirt and oils.

Immediately prior to welding, clean the first two or three sticks of the welding rod with acetone or denatured alcohol, using a clean, white lint-free cloth to wipe each stick of welding wire. From this point, do not touch the welding rod with your bare fingers or with dirty or oily gloves.

Welding Conditions—Where to Do the Welding

Do the welding in a clean, warm, well-lighted area that is free of wind or drafts from fans, opening doors, and open windows. Make sure that there are no liquid or solid combustibles in the welding area that could catch fire from sparks or arcs from your welding.

Welding in bright sunlight is far better

Left: These two pieces of ⁷⁄₈ x 0.032-inch tube are fitted perfectly, and the mill scale has been sanded off. Try to make every tubular joint fit like this.

Right: For angles greater than 45 degrees, some hand fitting still has to be done, as is shown on these two tubes for a race car suspension.

than welding in a dark room. You can see the weld seam and the weld puddle better in good lighting conditions.

Welds made in warm rooms, 80 degrees to 95 degrees Fahrenheit, are more likely to be good welds than those made in cold rooms. The parts you are welding should never be cold to your touch.

If you are welding parts that are ¹⁄₄-inch thick or thicker, you will have better luck if you preheat the parts to 250 degrees Fahrenheit, and if the part is ¹⁄₂-inch thick or thicker, be sure to preheat it to 350 degrees Fahrenheit in your kitchen oven for at least one hour before starting to weld. Try to block the part to be welded up off the steel of your welding table so the mass of the welding table will not pull the heat out of your weld assembly.

During and after welding, you may clean the weld area with a small stainless-steel wire brush. Do not brush the weld or the seam with a brush that has copper, brass, or aluminum bristles because the noncompatible bristles will transfer metal to the weld and will eventually cause the weld to crack.

The tube that angles up to the right in this picture has been poorly fitted. You can see the large gap that would surely be the cause of a crack in the weld if the tube is not replaced with one that fits properly.

Left: Mittler Brothers Machine and Tool makes this very heavy-duty tubing notcher that uses a milling cutter to notch the tubes for NASCAR-type roll cages.

Right: You will need to make lots of weld-on tabs like these to attach body panels, wiring harnesses, fuel lines, and many other things to your race car or airplane tubular structure.

Jigging

In the manufacturing and production business, the jigs that the parts are welded in are usually much heavier and more complex than the parts they produce. When you fabricate several units of a specific framework or assembly, a strong, intricate welding jig can significantly save time and materials.

If you are only making one or two units of a welded assembly, you can usually get by with a temporary lightweight jig. A pair of Vise-Grip pliers will often suffice, and several C-clamps are often the best way to clamp things together for welding. In this chapter, you will be shown several ways to jig parts together for welding. Then you can decide which of the pictured jigs will best suit your project.

Weld Table Jigs

You've probably noticed the artistic, polished stainless-steel boat railings on pleasure yachts and even some ski boats. One particular shop in Santa Barbara, California, designs boat railings for each individual boat and then fabricates the railings on a 4x8-foot welding table made of 3/8-inch steel plate.

It's easy to draw a layout on the top of a welding table with a black marker. After the layout and job are finished, the marker lines and notes can be removed with acetone.

Since each boat railing is unique, it would be too time consuming and expensive to build a welding jig for each one. Instead, the stainless-steel railing base plates are tack-welded to the tabletop, and the polished tubing (usually 1-inch

This plasma-cutter torch can cut pencil-fine lines in anything that is metallic, including aluminum and even stainless steel. It is the solution for cutting out stainless-steel exhaust flanges from 1/4-inch-thick stainless plate.

Several standard old methods of jigging your one-time welding projects include using the C-clamps, Vise-Grips, and metal clothespin–type clamps pictured here.

o.d. x 0.065-inch wall) is then formed, trimmed, and welded to each base plate.

After the railings are completely welded, the base-plate tack welds are cut off the welding tabletop with an abrasive cut-off wheel, the tack-weld spot is ground and polished smooth, and the new railing is taken out to the harbor and bolted to the deck of the yacht.

The tack welds on the welding tabletop are then ground away with a 4-inch hand grinder equipped with an 80-grit flap wheel. Next, the table is wiped down with acetone and prepared for the next boat-railing job. The temporary welding jig served its purpose and can be changed to fit any size and shape of boat deck.

Plywood Jigs

For many years—probably since the first steel-tube-fuselage airplane was built—welders have been building fuselage structures on plywood tabletops, much like how a stick-and-paper balsa flying model is built, except the framework on the model is glued rather than welded.

Take a look at the photos in this chapter to see how an airplane welding table is built. You will have to adjust the length and width of your plywood or particleboard welding table to suit your project, but the basic design will be the same.

Be sure that the height of the table is

Left: Simple 90-degree and 45-degree magnetic clamps will make your welding project easier. Buy several of these magnetic clamps.

Right: Williams Lo-Buck Tools makes this adjustable alignment tool that works great for many tubing and even-angle stock fit-ups.

Dr. Phil Royal built an aluminum plate and bolted an aluminum angle-welding jig so he could build several identical landing gear legs for his Osprey II seaplane.

Left: After the Osprey II landing gear leg was welded in the jig, it was sandblasted and powder coated to prevent rust when landing in the water.

Right: This particleboard and white pine welding jig ensures proper alignment when welding up the sides for a Finchbird experimental airplane.

An excellent fit-up of 4130 steel tubing members is evident in this picture. TIG or MIG welding can be done on this particleboard weld jig by clamping the ground to one of the tubes.

Top Left: After one side of the Finchbird airplane fuselage was tack welded with a gas welding torch, the frame was removed from the jig so the second side could be built on the jig.

Top Right: Wag-Aero Group, in Lyons, Wisconsin, is a typical aircraft weld repair shop. *Wag-Aero Group*

Bottom Left: A tack-welded 4130 steel-tubing airplane fuselage has been removed from its alignment jig for shipment to a customer, who will complete the welding on the tack welds, thereby saving several thousands of dollars in welding labor. *Wag-Aero Group*

Bottom Right: A RANS, Inc., aircraft welder is shown TIG welding a sub-assembly on a squaretube welding jig that ensures identical parts every time. *RANS, Inc.*

right so you'll have an easy stand-up welding layout. Kitchen cabinet work tops are designed for stand-up food preparation, so measure your kitchen cabinet-top height and make your plywood or particleboard table the same height.

After the table is built, you will need to level it for ease of measuring and setting up the tubular structure. Small, tapered wood shims can be used to level the base of the table to the floor. A hot glue gun or Bondo will hold the tapered shims in place on the floor.

Even if you plan to TIG or MIG weld your fuselage structure, the plywood or particleboard tabletop will work well. To make electrical contact with your framework, simply clip the welding-machine ground clamp to one of the main longerons or another part that will carry the welding current.

Don't spend too much time and money on plywood or particleboard welding tables unless you plan to build

several airplane fuselages to the same set of plans. Then you might take a little extra time to make the table more user-friendly.

Designing a Welding Jig

Often it is easier to build the first part to the dimensions on the plans and then simply make a jig to fit the first actual part. This is the design method used by many engineers who design welding jigs.

Another way to design a welding jig is to first cut out all the necessary parts from metal, fit them together, and then build a jig that will hold all the parts in place while they are welded. If the welded assembly is not too complicated, this method works pretty well.

Still another way to make a welding jig to fit a large structure—such as an airplane fuselage—is to design the welding jig from the blueprint that defines the fuselage. In one such case, I designed a rotatable welding jig for one of my airplane projects that defined the size and shape of the fuselage structure and at the same time provided a weld fixture for a

Top Left: This engine-mount welding jig was designed around the shape and actual size of the airplane firewall. Steel brackets locate the fire-wall mounting points.

Top Right: This light but rigid and strong welding jig ensures that every airplane fuselage built in this jig will be identical to the others. The jig is made from thin-wall square tubing. *RANS, Inc.*

Middle: A completed and painted airplane fuselage frame built in the welding jig shown in the photo above. *RANS, Inc.*

fuselage that measured 16 feet long, 4 feet wide, and 4 feet high.

That particular welding jig began with a 2½-inch-diameter, 0.080-inch wall tube, which was 20 feet long. At specific inch station locations along the length of the 2½-inch tube, fuselage bulkhead brackets were located. Then the bulkheads were attached to the brackets, and the longeron tubes were fitted to the bulkhead and tack welded in place.

As the fuselage assembly progressed, the 2½-inch tube provided a center point that allowed the fuselage structure to be rotated for ease of welding. As you likely know, the easiest and best welds are made flat, not uphill, not overhead, and not upside down. And, of course, the 2½-inch tube rotated in sawhorse-type frames at each end.

Ideas for Jigs

Take a close look at the numerous welding jigs in this chapter for ideas on how to design your particular welding jigs. There is no single, perfect way to design a welding jig, but each one you design will probably be better than your first. Just do it!

In order to ensure that dozens of Chevrolet V-6 engine mounts will fit on RV-6A kit airplanes, Jess Meyers of Belted Air Power, in Las Vegas, Nevada, builds each mount in this simple but strong angle-iron welding jig. *Belted Air Power*

MIG WELDING TIPS:

For easier welding, you should do the following:

- If at all possible, always weld in the flat position for better quality welds. This means not vertical, not horizontal, and for sure, not overhead.

- Never weld the "real" part until you have tested all the machine settings, amps, wire speed in fpm, gas flow, and especially weld accessibility.

- Always run a couple of test coupons on scrap material to make sure the machine settings and the operator are ready; notice that the welder (operator) is a big factor.

- Always use anti-spatter spray or dip jelly to prevent spatter buildup in the gun nozzle.

- Be sure to protect painted surfaces from smoke and spatter from the weld.

- Never MIG weld where pets or people can watch the arc. Ultraviolet light is emitted from the arc, and ultraviolet rays can cause eye cataracts and skin cancer over time. On a short-term basis, welding eye flash is painful; it causes late-night eye itching.

- When MIG welding stainless-steel sheet, be sure to back up the weld seam with copper strips or welder's ceramic-fiber paste to prevent atmospheric contamination in the weld.

- When MIG welding stainless-steel sheet tubing, always back-gas purge the inside of the tubing to prevent weld contamination.

- Be your own automatic "stitch timer" when welding thin metal, such as 0.020-inch to 0.050-inch thickness. Squeeze the trigger, weld a couple of seconds until you see a melt-through starting, then let up and let the weld cool and solidify for a couple of seconds, then squeeze the trigger and weld a couple of seconds more. Some of the biggest and best manufacturing companies weld tubular structures this way, with great results. Practice this procedure and you will soon develop the proper rhythm.

- Remember that dirt does not weld; clean your parts properly before welding.

- Always keep the MIG gun cable from being twisted and tangled. Never stand on the cable while you are welding. The reason is that the wire inside the cable will not feed smoothly if the cable is twisted or if you stand on the cable.

- Change the cups and the copper collets often; dirty cups and worn collets reduce the quality of the weld.

- Never watch the weld from behind the MIG gun because you can't see the puddle that way.

- Always watch the weld from the side of the MIG gun, where you will be able to see the wire melt off in the puddle.

- And most important of all, never be embarrassed if you have to cut out a bad MIG weld because it isn't sound. With a proper air-operated cutoff tool, it's not much trouble to cut out a bad weld on tubing. Then just re-do it properly.

OUT IN THE GARAGE

REPAIRING A REAR WINDOW CHANNEL

Welding is a great way to perform simple repairs. In this project, Eric Scarlett shows how to fix a rear window channel. When prepping 4130 steel, a thin film of rust is acceptable, but it needs to be free of paint, oil, and other contaminants. Clean the steel off with a liquid metal prep that contains phosphoric acid, available at auto body shops.

"One of the great things about welding is that if I mess it up, I can drag it back down and then put it back right. I can cut something in half, make it too short, cut it off again, and extend it a bit," Scarlett says. "Welding is not easy, but it can be fun when you do it right."

1: First grind the window channel in preparation for removal of the damaged section.

2: Then lay the channel window panel on a workbench and clamp it to 1x2-inch tubing to keep it flat.

3: The next step is to cut out the damaged section with a zap saw.

4: Here's what the window channel looks like after removing the damaged section.

5: After removing the damaged section, align the channel and smooth the rough edges with a sander.

6: Then hammer it straight.

7: Before going any further, remember to compare the old and new channels.

8: Then mark the cut lines.

9: Next check the cut lines for the splice.

10: When done cutting, see how the new section fits.

11: Using magnetic holders, secure the new section in place.

12: Then weld in the new section.

13: Next, clean up the repaired area with a grinder.

14: Eyeball the overall fit of the window channel.

15: Next, fit and tack in the new section and make your final welds.

16: Final welds.

17: With one more pass from the grinder, smooth out the body line.

18: Here is the new section, completely welded in place.

MEET THE PROS

Ed Federkeil

"Welding is an art."

Ed Federkeil, a fire captain, has managed to combine his 23-year firefighting career with two more interesting vocations: drag racing and custom truck fabrication. From the mid-1980s to mid-1990s, Federkeil was a regular on the NHRA tour, winning enough races to land a sponsored ride and some product endorsements. It was during his years of building and driving door slammers that Federkeil also began to do custom truck fabrication.

"The truck thing sort of happened by accident," Federkeil says. "A kid from California, who was one of the crew guys on Darryl Gwynn's top fuel team, was renting a room from me. He bought a half-ton pickup and started ordering mail order stuff for it—a lowering kit, custom wheels—all stuff that really wasn't that common on the East Coast back then. He kept telling me, 'Hey dude, why don't you start build-

ing trucks, man?' I thought he was crazy. I'm a drag racer; I don't fool with that stuff. Nobody would pay anything for that. Well, he built his truck in my race shop—and it was pretty cool—so he'd be driving it around and people would ask where they could get one, and he'd send them to me. I was turning them away, but after about 20 guys showed up—when the 21st came in—I said, 'Give me your keys. We're a truck shop.' It took me awhile, but I finally figured out there was a real market there."

Today Ed's company builds concept and feature vehicles for both Ford and General Motors for the annual Specialty Equipment Marketing Association (SEMA) show in Las Vegas.

"We build custom trucks; everything from luxury SUV conversions for athletes, celebrities, movie stars, to full air bag setups, to just about whatever anyone wants. I do stay away from things that I believe would not be safe, or from something that would diminish the value of the vehicle. There are guys in this field who are butchers. When I'm done, it's got to be functional, something I'd drive myself," he says.

"I know it's a cliché that you can do anything you want to if you want it bad enough, but it's true. It all depends how hard you want to work," he adds.

Ed Federkeil has done a lot of different kinds of fabrication projects over the years— everything from building a drag racing car to crafting a custom pickup truck. He also helped make an SUV into the ultimate tailgaiting machine.

MEET THE PROS

Lisa Legohn

"My weld is my signature."

Lisa Legohn became a welder because she thought it sounded like a cool—or rather hot—thing to do. As a 17-year-old student at Hollywood High, she heard about a welding vocational program through a school counselor, who told her the process was like "fire and a helmet." "I quickly told her to send me there," Legohn says.

Needless to say, she stuck with the program, graduated, and found a career in welding. In 1983 she started teaching welding part time at Compton Community College, and she ended up staying there for 20 years.

Legohn is known in the trade as one who is at the top of her game. So for anyone who wants to buy some welding equipment and learn the basics of the craft well enough to be comfortable doing various fabrication and repair jobs, Legohn is always willing to offer her expert advice.

"For most beginners the hardest thing to learn is patience. They'll probably use a lot of mild carbon steel, which melts anywhere from 2,300 to 2,500 degrees," she adds. "It doesn't melt instantaneously. It's not like a microwave oven. You have to allow the metal to melt. Have patience."

She's also quick to point out to those interested in making welding their full-time job that it is not an easy profession. "It's hot, you're going to sweat, you're at close range to 2,300-degree heat, you'll get burned. Believe me, it's not glamorous, and you're not going to get good at it overnight," she says. "There is no instant gratification; it takes a lot of practice."

She recommends that those looking for a career change first look to purchase a good home welding unit and get some practice. "Low-end units have a shorter duty cycle," she says, "which means you have to turn off the unit for a prescribed amount of time after so many hours or minutes of use before you can use it again. Generally, the cheaper the machine, the shorter the time it can be used continuously."

Legohn also likes to remind beginning welders that it takes almost the same amount of effort to make a junky weld as it does to make a quality weld, so it's always better to spend a little more effort making your welds perfect. "Think about all the bridges in the world, and all of the welds holding them together. A bridge to me is only as strong as its weakest weld," she says.

Other safety tips she often shares include the following: put your helmet on before striking an arc if you have an electric welding machine and remember that all types of welding involve extreme heat and things don't instantly cool down.

Welder extraordinaire Lisa Legohn is a welding instructor who loves her work.

MEET THE PROS

Eric Scarlett

"All these people say they're fabricators, they can do this or that—well, I can cook hamburgers, but I'm no chef."

First Class Autowerks is considered by many, including multiple award–winning designer/builder Doug Deberti, the place to go for custom air bag installations. The shop is also well known for innovative fiberglass work and custom restorations.

Like many of our other featured fabricators, Eric Scarlett, founder and owner of the company, began working on cars at an early age. His grandfather Joe Taormina came to America from Italy and, by the time Scarlett was born,

Eric Scarlett at his shop. He helped turn a 1984 Porsche 944 into a golf ball collector.

owned a gas station in Tarzana, California, a place Scarlett remembers well.

"Whenever we went to visit their house, I'd go into his garage and watch him work," Scarlett says. "I'd play with his tools, and it really got me into tinkering with toys and then with cars. He put my aunt and both of my uncles through college by working as a mechanic and that made an impression on me, that you could make money doing this."

As a young teenager, Scarlett took some woodworking and metal shop classes with a great teacher, which further sparked his interest in becoming a fabricator. "All of these things together put me into the mode of 'let's build it, let's do cars,'" he says. "After I learned the basics, I started hanging around with friends who had low-riders—hoppers with hydros. I actually lowered my first truck, a 1973 Datsun, when I was about 14."

Since that time, Scarlett has worked on everything from Ferraris and Lamborghinis to mini-trucks, vans, and at least one 1955 Olds Rocket 88 in his 17 years as a professional fabricator.

"I got started in fabrication by working at other shops to get the experience and soak up their knowledge," Scarlett says. "The guy who really taught me the most was Brian Jendro."

FIBERGLASS

F iberglass is versatile. It's also kind of messy, but the results are well worth it. Whether you're repairing or building from new, here are some tips you'll find handy.

"Fiberglass is always fun."
— Eric Scarlett, Episode 6 fabricator

Fiberglass, or fiber-reinforced plastic (FRP), has been used in thousands of products, not least of which is the Chevy Corvette, which has been clothed in a fiberglass body since its inception. While less durable than steel, it is lightweight and can be molded into almost any shape imaginable. If damaged, it can be easily patched and used with comparative ease. So for the home fabricator, it probably finds more use in automotive, motorcycle, and marine repair applications than any other function.

To use fiberglass resin, which is available in hardware stores, you must mix it with a catalyst in order for it to set up and harden. Once you've cut the proper-sized fiberglass mat or cloth, you apply a coat of resin with a brush, affix the mat, then cover it with another coat of resin. The number of coats you'll need depends on the nature of the job at hand. You can also easily mold fiberglass by soaking the mat in resin/catalyst, placing it into a shaped mold, and letting it harden. There are a number of different resin/catalyst combinations on the mar-

ket, each requiring a slightly different procedure for correct application, so an important rule in working with these materials is to carefully follow the manufacturer's instructions.

While there are no specific additional shop space requirements for using fiberglass, you need to ensure that you have adequate ventilation, as the materials involved can have harmful long-term health ramifications. The chemical components that make up the materials used when laying up fiberglass can cause everything from eye irritation to kidney disease to cancer. Always wear proper clothing, including gloves, to minimize contact with exposed skin, because some chemicals can be absorbed through the skin. Also, never work with fiberglass without wearing a respirator or a mask and some form of eye protection, preferably safety goggles.

"You can ruin your vision for life in less than a second," Rick Dobbertin says. "We seldom get second chances on this."

In addition to all of the above, keep in mind that many of these materials are highly flammable. Store your solvents and resins in their original containers and in a cool, well-ventilated place, as far from heat and sparks as possible.

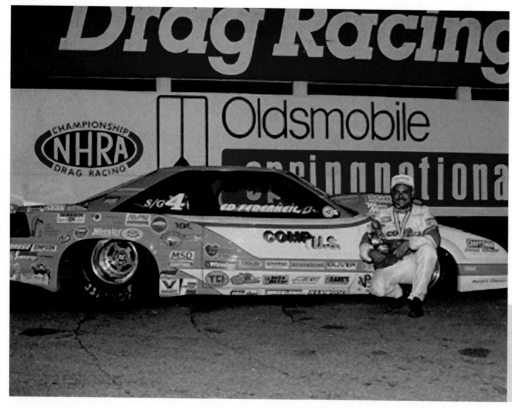

Fiberglass can be formed into any shape, and is a fairly versatile material to work with. However, it is relatively heavy and time consuming, as there need to be multiple layers of cloth and resin.

OUT IN THE GARAGE

BUILDING A FIBERGLASS STEREO ENCLOSURE

In addition to their other automotive fabrication projects, Eric Scarlett and his new partner, Jereme Elwell, do a lot of fiberglass work—not just the usual patching and other typical body repair work, but custom work in a variety of areas.

"I learned how to work with fiberglass by watching other people," Scarlett says. "The first thing I do if I have a big custom job is call in an expert. That's because fiberglass resins hurt my hands. Remember, when you work with fiberglass, you want to use a respirator and gloves."

In this fiberglass project, Scarlett and a colleague are placing a stereo system into the trunk of a 1955 Olds Rocket 88 that is being customized. It already has a full air bag setup, so now it needs some sounds.

"We'll have two 12-inch L7 speakers in the corners, an amp, and an equalizer on the floor, with a flush cover blending it all together into a single unit," Scarlett says. "I usually make an outer flush cover, something that will give you the right sort of look when you're done.

"With this kind of fiberglass enclosure, you've got to have a certain amount of air space, or the fiberglass will break from the bass moving the air inside the enclosure. For the speaker box enclosure we use MDF, medium-density fiberboard, not plywood," he adds.

For this project, you'll need some 4 x 8-foot fiberglass sheets, which are thin and can be bent almost in half. Other materials you'll need include a gallon of fiberglass resin, some tubes of resin hardener, fiberglass cloth (not matting, because the area you're working with is large), a lot of cheap paintbrushes, and plastic cups to dip them in.

"All stuff that can be thrown away when you're done," Scarlett says. "You'll also need a quart of acetone. Usually I tell people to buy a gallon, or even five gallons because it's so much cheaper. You can pick

1: This project begins with measuring and cutting pieces of medium-density fiberboard (MDF) to create a frame to hold stereo equipment and several air tanks inside the trunk.

up all the stuff you need at a home improvement store or any number of places. Don't get the cheapest stuff. Go for name brands."

Here's the complete list of materials you need to fabricate the fiberglass stereo enclosure:

- 1 (4 x 8) sheet of medium-density fiberboard (MDF)
- 2 (4 x 8 x $1/8$) sheets fiberglass bend board
- 1 gallon glass filler
- 1 gallon fiberglass resin and hardener
- 4 packages fiberglass cloths
- 1 gallon acetone
- 1 package cheap plastic drinking cups
- 4 yards speaker fleece
- 1 bag cheap (2-inch) paintbrushes
- 1 quart fiberglass primer and hardener
- dual-action stick-back sandpaper and long, flat board sandpaper in 36-, 80-, and 120-grit gauges
- miscellaneous fiberglass spreaders
- miscellaneous $1^1/_2$-inch drywall screws

In order to make your final product look as good as an expert's, Scarlett offers this advice: "Like a lot of people, I used to use chicken wire or foam to shape what I was going to do and then laid plastic over it— trash can plastic or whatever—and then put all the fiberglass over it. What my guy uses is speaker fleec- ing, the stuff that covers speaker gratings. You can buy it in upholstery shops. It cuts easily with a razor blade."

2: This square rack will hold the amp.

In this approach, you stretch the fleecing over the fiberboard and fiberglass enclosure, then staple it in place to angled corners. Then you start dipping your resins and putting the actual matting onto the fleecing.

"Once it hardens up, you start building your material—how high you want it, how thick. Then you start sanding it and take out any imperfections," Scarlett says. "We start sanding with a 36-gauge and get progressively finer until it's totally smooth. Then it's just a matter of building it up and sanding it down until you're satisfied that it's smooth enough. I like it to be as smooth as a mirror. Then, at the end, we prime and paint it to match the car. It's a process that takes some time, but it's worth it."

Now the installed components are in place, including two 5-gallon air tanks, two 2500 class amps, two capacitors, one 300-amp fuse and fuse holder, and wiring. The enclosure is in primer. When the car is painted, the enclosure will be painted and detailed to match.

For anyone setting up their own small fabrication shop, Scarlett recommends the following:

- a complete set of quality hand tools
- both metric and standard
- a torch set
- a name-brand MIG welder
- a top-quality 6-horsepower
- 60-gallon air compressor
- miscellaneous hand grinders and sanders
- jack stands
- a vise
- a good, strong workbench

Scarlett also has some final words of advice for those contemplating their own fiberglass project: "If you're just getting into fiberglass, I'd suggest you start by patching something small in order to get used to working with the materials."

3 and 4: Next, measure and cut the MDF to fit around the air tanks.

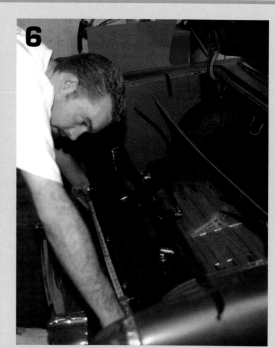

5: Cut the Masonite to fit around the front of the trunk opening.

6: Always check your fit before you go on to making the next cut.

7: Gather the materials needed for the project.

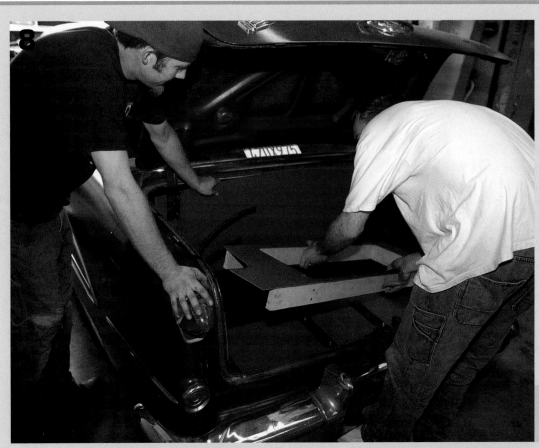

8: Test-fit components as you go, making sure your cuts are accurate.

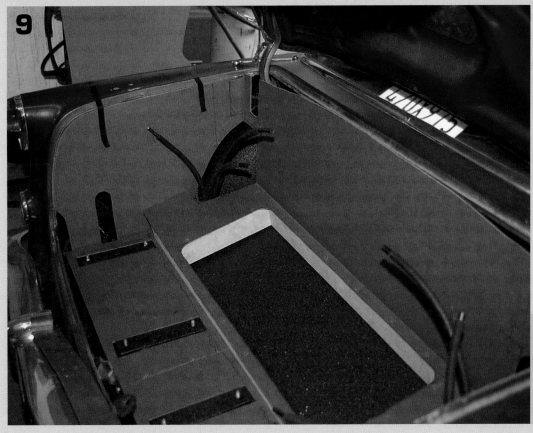

9: The rack is now ready to be prepped before being fiberglassed. Scuff the material with 36-grit sandpaper so resin and fiberglass will adhere.

10: Apply fiberglass fleece to the corners. The fiberglass will adhere to the surface, giving it the desired shape. Right, you see the fleece being stapled tightly in place.

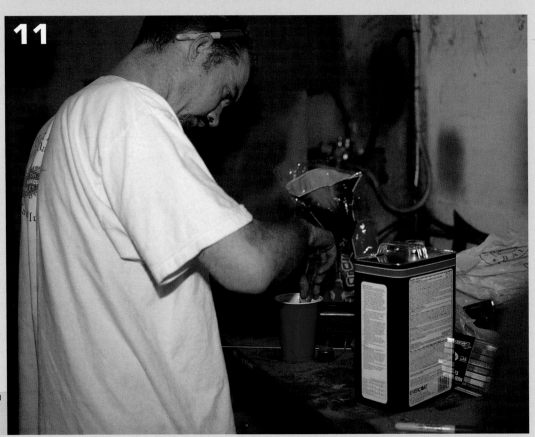

11: Then mix the resin with the hardener tube.

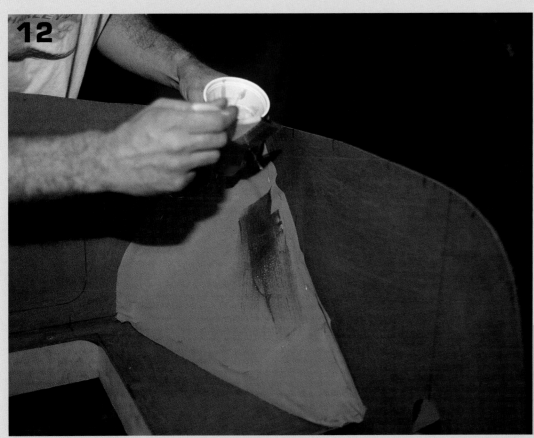

12: Apply thick layers of resin for strength. You must brush it on thoroughly so that it soaks through the mat. Also soak it into the wood/masonite for adhesion.

13: Lay the dry fiberglass mat over the wet resin and work the mat into the resin.

14: Work the resin through the mat with a Bondo scraper to avoid lumps.

15: Then apply more resin. Note that about halfway through the drying process, you should trim the rough edges away with a razor. If you wait until it's fully dry, you'll need a saw.

16 and 17: Add mat and resin to the back side. Note that you'll want to double-coat corners for strength, and sand everything smooth with a power sander before applying the fiberglass reinforced auto body filler.

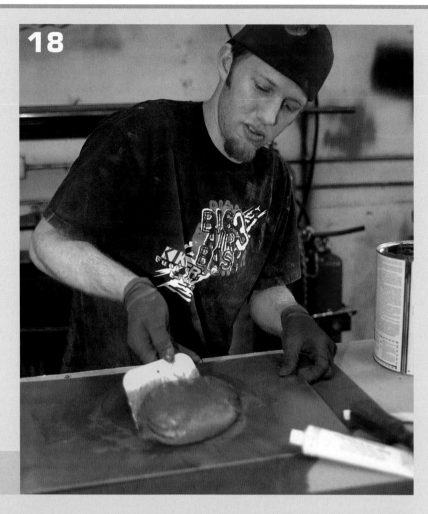

18: Mix the fiberglass-reinforced auto body filler with hardener on a flat surface, as shown.

19: Spread the filler on the enclosure surface to make it smooth and build it up.

20: Then file the reinforced auto body filler to get a semi-smooth finish. This will also remove air pockets, which you can fill with another coat of glass.

21: After filling (or cheese grating) the glass, add another coat. Keep up this process until the surface is smooth.

22: If you need to shape the glass to a curve, sand it with a socket.

23: Sand with a hand grinder until you have a perfect surface. You can do final touchup sanding with sandpaper.

24: Here you see the enclosure unit ready for installation.

25: Here is the finished product with the air tanks, subwoofers, and amps installed.

Chapter 6
MACHINING

Sometimes you need a part that doesn't exist. But, because you're resourceful, skilled — and because you read this chapter — you can make it yourself.

**"Don't try to over-engineer everything— reinventing the wheel. Make it simple and chances are you'll make it work."
— Al Teague, hot rod builder**

While the ability to machine parts will give you more capability to do certain types of jobs, it is not essential for most small fabrication shops, any more than a sheet metal brake would be needed by someone who only makes parts for his HO-gauge model railroad. But if you really want to get into machining, the most common piece of equipment you'll add to your shop is a lathe.

The historical importance of the lathe, which makes accurate machining of cylindrical parts possible, cannot be underestimated. Today's lathes may bear but scant resemblance to those original units, but the principles of operation are essentially unchanged.

A lathe for a small fabrication shop should be a compact but versatile unit. These are often referred to as "hobby lathes" due to their ability to turn out small precision parts for things like scratch-built models. Before you buy a lathe, consider carefully what you intend to use it for. Just as it's easier to paint a soapbox derby racer than a top race car, it's easier, and more economical, to do small machining jobs on a small lathe.

If it makes sense for your workload and budget, adding a vertical milling machine for machining flat surfaces, precision drilling, hollowing out, and other operations not associated with the lathe will give you the kind of versatility not usually found outside a professional fabrication shop.

Some large fabrication shops have fully computerized CAD/CAM capabilities. This permits a part to be designed on the computer in 3-D and then precision machined by computer-controlled lathes and milling machines. While this expensive technology might seem well beyond the scope of most small fabrication shops, that is no longer necessarily the case, at least for certain types of jobs. Recent developments in the field have now made it possible for fabricators with basic computer skills to design parts on their PCs, have them precision manufactured, often half a world away, and delivered to their doors.

To see just how this process works, an experiment was set up based on the fol-

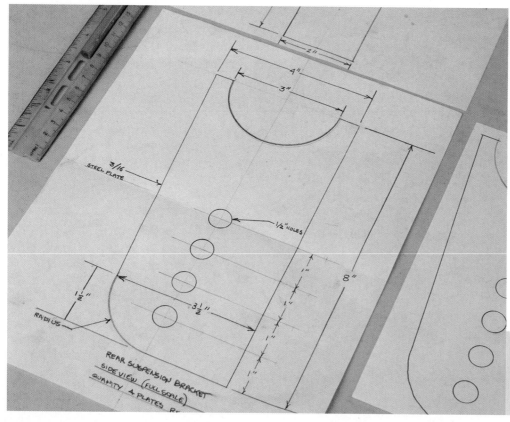

These are the plans in a more traditional fashion, as Joe Barnes drew the bracket on a 1-to-1 scale on paper before trying to fabricate it. *David Pruitt*

lowing: A stock car spins out on a race-track, slams into the wall tail first, and inadvertently becomes the trigger mechanism for our fabrication test. Among the parts damaged in the crash were two rear suspension mounting brackets. The car, now undergoing a rebuild by its new owner/driver, Joe Barnes, would, as he notes, need replacements for the damaged parts.

"The rear end lower mounting brackets are also home for the coil-over shocks," Barnes says. "They are mounted to the lower part of the quick change rear end. The handling of the car is greatly dependent on the accuracy of the suspension mounting points."

Since the bracket is a custom item not available at your local parts supply store, it would have to be fabricated—in this case by Barnes and his shop assistant, Greg Scigliano.

Making Parts on Your Own

Fabricating a suspension bracket job is a straightforward process, Barnes explains, involving many basic techniques that apply to your own projects.

"First, make drawings of the bracket to be replaced. Greg and I did the job using regular shop tools and equipment," Barnes says. "We primarily used a ruler and basic mechanical drawings, then we used a drill press, saw, grinder, welder, and plasma cutter to do the rest of the work."

After making the drawing, the next step in fabricating the suspension brackets was to cut a 3-inch radius section out of a $\frac{1}{8}$ x 4-inch piece of flat steel using a hole saw or plasma cutter.

"We located the centerline, then sawed

Here he transfers the plans to flat steel. *David Pruitt*

the hole, then cut the piece in half. Because a chop saw takes $1/8$ inch out, we allowed $1/16$ inch extra to allow for what the blade cuts out. The next step was to take a center punch and mark the center point for the hole saw, then drill what's called a pilot hole," Barnes adds. "We had a very defined centerline, so we drilled the pilot hole, then switched to the hole saw for the big hole."

Once the hole was finished, Barnes and Scigliano cut the piece to the proper length using two-piece sections so that when it's split in half, all four pieces will be cut with the half circle already in place. Then they cleaned up all imperfections.

"The trick to doing a really clean job is to clamp on some kind of guide so that you have something to follow, rather than try to do it freehand," Barnes said. "This could also be done with an oxyacetylene torch if you don't have a plasma cutter. The only real difference would be in the amount of cleanup work needed."

After tacking the four brackets together, Barnes laid out the four suspension mounting points, bolting the spacers and rod ends where they would go. "In order to make sure the brackets were mounted perpendicular to the pinion gear, we used an angle finder and a level," he says.

While not part of his original bracket plans, Barnes then welded an 8-inch section of 2 x 2-inch, 120-square tubing on to the suspension brackets. This tubing

Here is a view of a downloaded race car suspension bracket, which is drawn in 3-D through an online part design program. *David Pruitt*

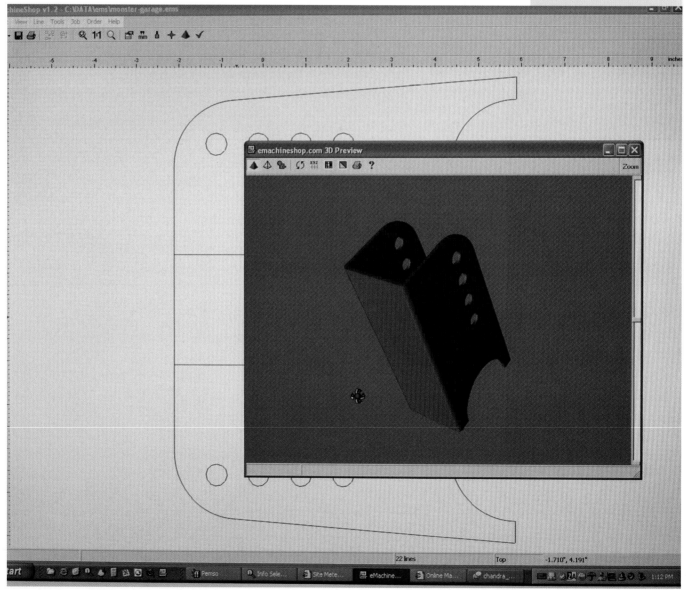

will be used to mount the coil-over shock assembly. Some modern production cars use a somewhat similar design in that their springs and shocks are behind the rear axle.

Making Parts on Your PC

After a short break for some much-needed coolants, Barnes was ready to tackle the suspension bracket job all over again—on his laptop. He visited the eMachineShop.com website to download the CAD drawing software to design the part. Then he built the part online and compared it with the bracket he built in terms of build quality, cost, time, and so on. (Other websites offer similar services.)

"You put it all together, using some simple commands, and then you select your material, the desired thickness, and if you're designing a complex 3-D shape, you set the height that's the third dimension of the drawing," Jim Lewis, president and founder of the business, says.

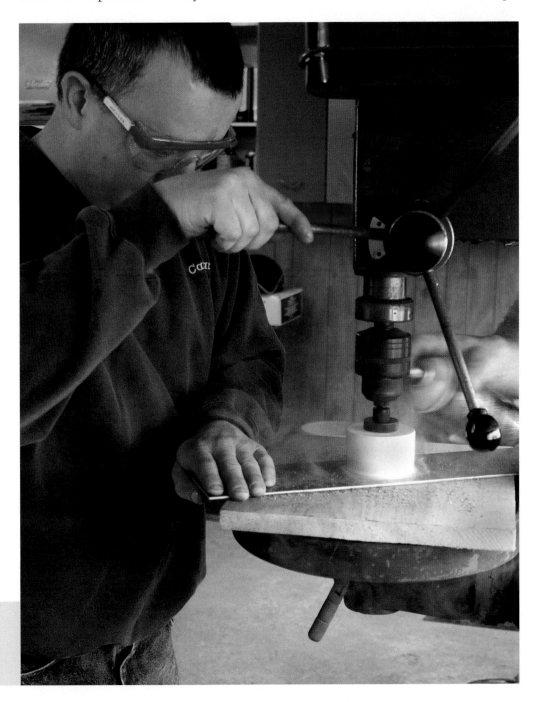

If you're making a part the old-fashioned way, the next step after drawing out the plans is to cut the bracket's radius section with a hole saw. *David Pruitt*

Make the next cut with a chop saw. *David Pruitt*

"Then go to the 3-D view and actually see that your part is what you intended it to be. The software is designed for easy use by someone with some engineering knowledge and for the total amateur who's just getting into it and doesn't know anything about manufacturing."

The downloaded software also gives warning messages about things such as certain manufacturing restrictions. For instance, if you're doing a sheet metal piece and you're bending it too close to the edge because you just want a little

ridge, the software will tell you that the bend line is too close to the edge and you can't do that; instead it will recommend a distance to make the design work. Then you make a change, or changes, until you get it right.

Rather than follow all of the necessary steps used to order the brackets, below are some of the main points.

With the software installed, Barnes went to the "shop menu" and selected .118-inch steel for the bracket, as this was the closest to his original specs.

Grind off the suspension
bracket's rough edges.
David Pruitt

He clicked on the rectangle button, then clicked on the starting and ending points of the rectangle, went up to the numeric bar, and entered the dimensions of 8 x 4 inches.

The next step was the "line menu" where he selected "machine," then selected a laser cutter to perform the work.

Following the on-screen prompts, Barnes drew a 180-degree arc onto the rectangle, then put the four half-inch-diameter holes and the tapered sides into place, giving him roughly the shape of one side of the bracket.

Back to the toolbar: he clicked on "rectangle," selected the upper part of the design, then entered edit-copy-edit-paste, pulled down the control key to drop the top down to the bottom, making a mirror image to complete the bracket template in 2-D. He then entered an "ungroup" command to delete any extra segments (this is the computer's version

of cleaning up any imperfections left after cutting a piece of steel), selected the two horizontal lines, then went to the "line machine" command and selected bend, 90 degrees.

The bracket design completed, Barnes entered the 3-D command in order to study the bracket from different angles. His request for a price for two of the brackets was answered in seconds: $128.17, including tax and shipping. The brackets would be delivered within 22 days.

When the brackets arrived at his shop, Barnes gave them two thumbs up.

"I think these and the ones I made will do exactly the same job," he says. "The accuracy is exactly the same. The website-designed ones are bent rather than three pieces welded together, which makes for a cleaner, neater job. I think what's nicer about these is that I didn't have to spend four hours of my time doing the fabrication."

Top: Cut through the center-line to create the bracket's half circles. *David Pruitt*

Left: Eliminate any imperfections with the grinder again. *David Pruitt*

Right: Using a metal slug from the hole saw as a template, draw out the pattern. *David Pruitt*

Bottom: Use a plasma cutter to get the correct angle. *David Pruitt*

Left: Next mark the suspension mounting points on the four brackets. *David Pruitt*

Bottom: Here Greg drills the four brackets together for exact accuracy. *David Pruitt*

MEET THE PROS

Jim Lewis

"If you can get the concept drawn, we can probably build it."

For Jim Lewis, who has always tinkered with things mechanical and who holds a degree in computer science, eMachineShop.com was the result of his quest to combine two of his favorite things.

"I've been playing with mechanical things since I was a little kid," Lewis says. "I was always taking things apart and then trying to put them back together again. Sometimes I succeeded. Over the years I've built up a collection of tools in my shop at home, but it was when I got my first machine tool, a hobby lathe, and saw how that dramatically increased the capabilities of what I could accomplish that I began to think

about combining my machine background and the computer science background. I also had a pretty strong interest in Internet business models. So I put them all together and came up with my website business."

It took more than seven years for the website to be fully operational, as the software needed to design parts took some years to create. With an official launch in 2004, the website has received orders from all around the world.

"We do a lot of parts that are transportation-oriented: automobiles, motorcycles, bicycles, airplanes," Lewis says. "We've even had orders from NASA."

Jim Lewis combined two of his loves—machining and computers—to create a successful fabrication business that makes many projects easier for the do-it-yourselfer.

MEET THE PROS

Joe Barnes

"No one was going to give me a race car, so I had to learn to build my own."

Like Lewis, Joe Barnes has always been involved with things mechanical, but for Barnes the computer is just another tool learned out of necessity rather than a passion.

"I've always been into cars and racing," Barnes says. "My dad took me to stock car races when I was a kid. My uncle had an auto repair shop, so I sort of grew up around mechanical things. When I was about nine, I disassembled and reassembled a lawnmower engine. I started working with my uncle when I first got my driver's license, then worked at some other shops and for a Ford dealership. In 1988, I bought my own shop. What really inspired me to stick with it was the fact that I love racing."

Barnes built his first race car in 1984 but didn't really get serious about it until 1989, when he built a car to race on the tracks in New England. Even though he had some success, the money and time he spent away from his family prompted him to stop racing and concentrate on his garage business.

Now that his children are older and the business is flourishing, he is starting up again and is in the process of rebuilding the car for which the brackets in this project were fabricated.

Joe Barnes comparing the online-designed bracket to his hand-fabricated part.

MEET THE PROS

Al Teague

"The more you work at it, the more you'll learn."

On August 21, 1991, a southern California hot-rodder named Al Teague did what many believed would never be done by driving a single-engine, wheel-driven car across the Bonneville Salt Flats at a two-way average speed of 409.986 miles per hour. Although it's true that others, such as Craig Breedlove, Art Arfons, Gary Gabelich, Don Vesco, and Andy Green, have gone faster, they did it in turbine- or jet-powered vehicles, which were more aircraft than automobile. Today, some years later, Teague's record still stands.

The contrast between the current out-

right LSR record-breaking car, which broke not only the record but the sound barrier as well, and Teague's *Spirit of '76* effort is equivalent to the difference between Lindbergh's *Spirit of St. Louis* and the space shuttle. How was it possible for one man, working with only basic fabricating tools in a small garage behind his mother's house, to build a car without major corporate sponsorship dollars and drive it into the record books? Let's see.

"Basically the car was built with regular hand tools, a drill press, a small air compressor, an oxyacetylene welder and

One of the fastest men on the planet at work in his office, preparing for a record run. *Thomas "Pork Pie" Graf*

torch set, and an old reciprocating saw that I bought for $40," Teague says. "The car evolved over a number of years from its beginnings as an open-wheel lakester with a 150-inch wheelbase. The wheelbase was next lengthened to 180 inches, and finally to the 225-inch wheelbase streamliner with the wheels enclosed that set the record. We had to move the rear wheels closer together to enclose them into the body, took the front axle and front end off, then made a new one where the wheels sit slightly offset instead of beside each other, something that had never been done before."

Although the body liner was completed in 1982, the Bonneville course had been closed due to wet weather, and it wasn't until 1984 that this car made its initial runs on the salt, turning 268 miles per hour. That was followed the next year—the last with the blown 392-ci Chrysler cast-iron hemi—with a 353-miles-per-hour run. The next power plant, an aluminum alloy hemi race engine, provided more speed: 384 miles per hour in 1988, 398 miles per hour in 1989, and 400 miles per hour in 1990. The record of 409.277 set by the Summers brothers' multi-engine *Goldenrod* in 1965 was now in Teague's sights.

Hidden under the sleek fiberglass skin of Teague's *Spirit of '76* is as fine an example of dedication and problem-solving skills as you are ever likely to come across. Fabricated entirely by hand, without benefit of wind tunnels, computer models, or major sponsorship dollars, this purpose-built car did the job it was intended to do and put its builder into the history books. Here's what went into building the 27-foot, 9-inch-long, 4,500-pound machine:

A small high-speed parachute that's used to get the car down to about 300 miles per hour. "The bottom holds the big chute, which then gets deployed to bring the car to a stop, with some help from the rear brakes," Teague says.

A transaxle out of a 1969–70 mid-engine Indy car, set up like a sprint car, with a Chevy 12-bolt ring and pinion in it.

"The entire car was built in a 20 x 20-foot garage. I started on the lakester version of the car New Year's Day 1975 and worked on it every day after my regular job until it was ready to go to Bonneville in August 1976," Teague adds. "Until that trip, it never left the garage."

A data equipment recorder that monitors engine functions like blower pres-

The conversion from lakester to streamliner takes shape as thin strips of veneer are fastened in place, then covered with fiberglass cloth and sealant to produce the body mold. *Al Teague*

sure, oil pressure, and pan pressure, and monitors the cylinder head temps two or three times a second.

"The frame is basically just rectangular tubing put together kind of like when you built model airplanes when you were a kid and you put the sticks together and the pins—this was before the plastic ones—and we just shaped it," Teague says. "It's really strong, but it does flex some."

Even Teague would probably agree that if there is one part of the car in which inspiration outdid perspiration, it is with the placement of the front wheels.

"The FIA rules say you have to have a minimum of four wheels with two of them on a common axle; it has to be driven by a minimum of two and steered by a minimum of two, and they can't all be in one line," Teague says. "Since I didn't want a wide bulge in the front bodywork covering the wheels, like most liners had back then, I had to figure out a way to get the wheels side by side but really close together, and still have room for an axle and kingpin and all that stuff. Then I thought: What if I just moved one of them back a bit? That would open up enough room for everything. I remembered walking by a heavy equipment yard and noticing how they mounted the articulated wheels on mobile cranes and that image somehow stuck with me. Then I had to figure out how to steer it."

One night, while lying in bed, he came up with an answer: building a steering similar to a modern airplane bell crank. "I anchored it like a Ford I-beam suspension with a Dodge van steering gear shaft that turns a butterfly-type Pittman arm hooked up to a pair of drag links attached to two $1^{1}/_{2}$-ton truck spindles with torsion bar suspension over it and two radius rods," Teague says. "It worked, and it'll turn 20 degrees, whereas most liners only turn two or three. I can make a U-turn with it, which makes a big difference when you're going for an FIA record run because you only have one hour to get turned around and do all your maintenance for the return run, so any time saved is a big help."

Teague got into cars through his older brother, Harvey, who was mechanically inclined and started getting the first hot rod magazines back in the late 1940s. "He would buy old cars for $10, bring them home, and take them apart," Al says. "Of course, we never had the money to fix them. My dad would get them running if he could. About 1948, Dad started taking us to the motorcycle speedway races over at Lincoln Park in Los Angeles. Once I smelled the Castrol on those JAP engines, that was it.

"Everybody we hung around with back then was into cars. We started going to drag races in the mid-1950s, and about 1958 I got my own car and fixed it up—put a '56 Chevy engine in it, painted it. Harvey and I bought a roadster together and took it to the drags every weekend.

He began to lose interest, then he went into the service, and I took it over."

In the late 1960s, after spending time in the Army himself, Al started going to Bonneville. In 1972, he got behind the wheel of a B/Fuel open cockpit '29 Model A highboy roadster that turned 268 miles per hour. "I raced the highboy until the lakester was ready to run in 1975," Teague says. "I ran the car as a lakester until 1981, when it set a fast time of 308 miles per hour, then started the work of turning it into a streamliner. I'm actually rebuilding the roadster again here at the shop, something to have some fun with."

As someone who has worked as a machinist and millwright, taught machine shop, engine building, and high-performance tuning classes and built the fastest single-engine car in the world, Al Teague knows a thing or three about what it takes to become a good fabricator.

"If you're just starting out and want to set up your own shop at home or what-ever, I'd recommend you start with a good set of tools, a MIG welder, a good drill press, a small flat steel grinder, and then a little later on, a small lathe and a tap and die set," Teague says. "When you're building something, don't let little things stop you. If you don't know how to do something, chances are that someone will step in and give you a hand and pretty soon things will start coming together. Don't try to over-engineer everything—reinventing the wheel. Make it simple and chances are you'll make it work."

He also says that many people under-estimate their abilities, figuring that they can't complete harder fabrication jobs. "Well, just try it and see," he says. "You might be surprised."

He's even surprised himself once in a while, like the time he went out on the salt in October 2002, and set another 400-plus FIA world record. You'll no doubt find him back at Bonneville again once the roadster is finished.

Heading for the measured mile and a drive into the record books. Both the car and its trailer are handmade with all American parts. *Leon Braskamp*

HYDRAULICS AND PNEUMATICS

Pressure and liquid or pressure and gas, can supply you with great leverage. While the actual systems can get complex, the principles behind them are quite simple.

Computer-generated image of the frame for a mechanical shark. Hydraulics, controlled by a person inside the frame, will make the finished product swim realistically. Read more about this project in chapter eight.

"On the first day, Jesse made a comment about how I had the coolest hydraulics he had ever seen. That was assurance enough for me."
— Todd Blandford, hydraulics expert

Hydraulics involves the science of controlling and using water pressure or the pressure of other fluids and fluid mechanics to address engineering problems. In cars, the most common use of hydraulic systems is in the brakes, where as you push the brake pedal, the pedal pushes fluid through the brake lines and against a piston, which in turn pushes on the brake pads or shoes and stops the car.

Hydraulics often involve the use of a pump to generate pressure and move the fluid, and a cylinder, which the fluid acts against and causes to move. These pumps come in many shapes and sizes. Some are capable of generating a lot of pressure with a low volume of fluid, while others use a high volume of fluid but a low pressure. Pumps will typically have two ports on them and the fluid will be pumped out of one port, while the fluid returning from the cylinder will

flow back to the pump through the other. Some pumps are bidirectional, meaning they are capable of pumping fluid out of either port, while some are only capable of pumping out of one.

Pumps can operate on either DC or AC current, but Todd Blandford, a hydraulics expert, says he's only used DC pumps in his work. He also says that he likes to be able to adjust the pressure output of the hydraulics pump.

"With the pumps I use, which are bidirectional, I'm able to adjust the pressure coming out of each port individually, meaning I can have two different pressure settings, giving me more control over my system," he says.

Cylinders, sometimes called actuators, also come in many sizes and shapes. The cylinder has two ports on it, just like the pump, one at either end of the cylinder. It also has a rod that comes out of one end. Internally, that rod is connected to a piston.

"And depending on which port the fluid is coming in at, that will determine the direction of movement of the rod," Blandford says. He adds that the diameter of the piston or "bore" of the cylinder is another important factor. "The larger the bore, the larger the internal piston," he says. "The larger the piston, the more surface area it has, meaning more fluid can push against it, creating more force."

The other power factor in the cylinder is its stroke, or how far the rod moves out of the cylinder. This will determine how far you can actually move something. Since the rod comes out of the cylinder, a seal must be used around the rod so it doesn't leak. This seal is what usually determines the cylinder's overall pressure rating. Pressures over the rated capabilities of the cylinder will result in leaks.

One other note: Always pay attention to the rod diameter itself. If a too-small rod diameter pushes against heavy loads, the rod could "bow" as it comes out of the cylinder, possibly ruining the cylinder.

Equally important is the diameter of the lines, as well as the fitting size used. Make sure the line and fitting diameter will complement your pump fluid output. Using a pump capable of 10 gallons a minute with $\frac{1}{8}$-inch lines and fittings would be a waste of a pump. Likewise, using $\frac{1}{2}$-inch lines with a 1-gallon-a-minute pump would be equally wasteful.

The tricky part of figuring out a hydraulics system is matching the capa-bilities of the pump against the capabilities of the cylinder so that your setup moves what you want and as fast as you want it to. The following are items to take into consideration when setting up a hydraulics system:

The bore of the cylinder: This will determine how much force the cylinder can generate and, indirectly, how fast a cylinder will move based on pump output.

The stroke of the cylinder, which will determine how far an object will be moved.

The fluid output of the pump, which will determine how fast a cylinder fills.

The pressure the pump can generate.

So, how do you figure out how all of these components work together to create a well-functioning system? Here's our basic formula:

$$\text{Force} = \text{Pressure} \times \text{Area}$$
$$\text{or}$$
$$F = P \times A$$

Force is the result, pressure is the operating system pressure, and area is the area of the cylinder piston. Incidentally, most cylinders are round, since a round shape is easier to seal. That said,

Hydraullic systems can be made to move just about any-thing, from disc brake calipers to mechanical sharks.

the formula for figuring a round area is:

$$Area = pi \times (Radius)2$$

If you plug that into the formula above, you get:

$$F = P \times (pi \times R2)$$

Putting that formula to the test, let's say you want to lift something straight up that weighs 125 pounds and you have an operating pressure of 500 psi. So far, you have:

$$F = P \times A$$

$$F = 125$$
$$P = 500$$

$$125 = 500 \times A$$

$$125/500 = A$$

$$0.25 = A$$

Then remember that A equals (pi x R2), so 0.25 = (pi x R2)

When you divide .25 by pi, you get .079 or thereabouts (see below).

$$R2 = 0.079$$

The square root of .079 is .282, making our radius a bit over 0.25 inch (0.282, to be precise):

$$R = 0.282$$

So, if you chose a cylinder with a bore of 0.5 inches (which means the radius is 0.25 inches), and a working pressure of 500 psi, the force would be 98.17 (see below), which is not enough to lift 125 pounds.

$$F = 500 \times pi \times (0.25)2$$
$$F = 98.17$$

Todd Blandford, though, doesn't typically use a cylinder with a bore smaller than 0.75 inch. So if you used a bore of 0.75 inches, your force would come out to F = 220.88, which would be plenty to lift 125 pounds. With a 1-inch-bore cylinder, the force would equal 392.69.

Now, let's look at how an increase in the pressure instead of the cylinder bore changes the formula. Staying with a $\frac{1}{2}$-inch-bore cylinder but increasing the operating pressure to 1,000 psi results in a force of 196.34, which would also lift 125 pounds.

Now let's compare this another way:

Our original design called for a 0.5-inch-bore cylinder with an operating pressure of 500 psi, resulting in F = 98.17.

By doubling the cylinder bore to 1 inch with an operating pressure of 500 psi, the force reached 392.69.

Yet doubling the pressure to 1,000 psi with a 0.5-inch cylinder bore resulted in F = 196.34:

$$F = 1000 \times pi \times (.025 \times .025)$$
$$F = 196.34$$

As you can see, increasing the cylinder size had more of a profound effect on our system. If room for the cylinder is no problem, it's more effective to increase the bore. With the 1-inch-bore cylinder, you could actually decrease the operating pressure and achieve the same results. A lower operating pressure is always a good thing, as you stand a better chance for a leak-free system for a longer period of time, as well as an increase in the lifespan of your components. If your cylinders are rated for 825 psi, it's much better to run your system at 500 psi than 800 psi.

Hydraulics: What Are They Really Good For?

You can use hydraulics in a ton of applications.

If something can be moved, nine times out of 10, hydraulics can move it. So the question ultimately becomes this: Is it practical to use hydraulics to move this object? It's a question only the person contemplating the project can answer. To look at ways you can use hydraulics in fabrication projects, we'll outline one that is a more common application and another that is a custom application.

OUT IN THE GARAGE

BUILDING A LOG SPLITTER

One simple yet effective use of hydraulics is in a homemade log splitter. Here's how to make one:

First, buy a tractor cylinder from a local farm supply store, then build the track and mounts and plumb the hydraulics using premade lines from a local hydraulic vendor. Choose a cylinder with a 4-inch bore and a 24-inch stroke. The distance between the pushing platform and the cutting edge is about 26 inches, so the pushing platform will never "bottom" against the cutting edge. The tractor pump generates about 2,500 psi, resulting in a whopping 31,415 pounds of force.

You can complete this project rather cheaply if you didn't need a pump. Use the internal pump of a tractor. The cylinder will cost about $150, which includes the heavy-duty clevis mounting ends. Lines run about $120, which includes tees and quick disconnects to splice off of the tractor pump lines. The cam followers cost about $60 and the steel about $20, not including the H beam. The control valve is about $75. Throw in $50 for paint and miscellaneous and that brings our total to about $500. Now, go out and price one. Typically they run anywhere from $800 to $1,200. Even with the cost of a pump (if you don't have a tractor), you could build this unit for less than the price of a new one.

This base of the log splitter is a 6-foot length of $1/4$-inch-thick H beam. The cutting edge sits at one end of the unit, while the cylinder and pushing platform are mounted at the other. The directional control valve sits atop the unit. *Ben Ganey*

This is the business end, or pushing platform. The "points" you see are nothing more than bolts screwed through the piece and sharpened. These are to hold the log while pushing. *Ben Ganey*

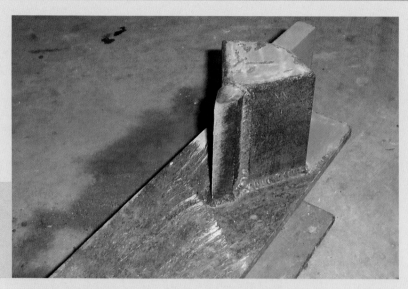

Right: The cutting edge of the unit is made up of an 8-inch length of 1 x 5-inch flat stock, ground to an edge. Two pieces of 2 x 3 x ¼-inch angle are turned on end and welded to the blade for support, as well as to help split the log. There is a ¼-inch cap welded on top of the angles. *Ben Ganey*

The pushing platform is made of three pieces of 1 x 5-inch material, roughly 7 inches long. Gussets made from ¼-inch material have been added for support. The platform rides on the top of the H beam using cam followers. One cam follower is positioned to ride on the top, while two more cam followers are positioned to ride on the bottom edge of the top surface.

This valve controls the direction of the cylinder. Pushed back, it will direct fluid to retract the cylinder; pushed forward, it will move the cylinder rod out. It also has a neutral position, allowing fluid to simply flow through the valve with no movement of the cylinder.

INSTALLING A HYDRAULIC DOOR ACTUATOR

The second hydraulics project involves opening and closing an automobile door. In the custom automotive field, this used to be handled by electric actuators. But these were often slow, bulky, and sometimes just plain expensive if you had some heavy work for it to do. Todd Blandford has used hydraulics on a number of car door systems and has been able to create systems that open a rear hatch in as little as two to three seconds and close it in three to four seconds. The typical electric actuator would take twice or sometimes three times that long.

For this project, the first step is to examine where you might want to mount the cylinder. For this example, Blandford is working with opening a typical front car door. He likes to mount the cylinder under the front dash, with the rod end attached to the moving surface. This location will keep the cylinder tucked away from the passenger area.

The next step involves figuring out how long a stroke you will need to open the door. To do this, pick a spot on the door, (Blandford usually chooses a spot near the hinge point) and mark it. Then, use a coat hanger that has been taped to the dash to measure the distance from the fully opened door to the mark on the door.

Next, it's time to make some mounts. The door mount is easier to make than the dash mount. Blandford often uses a simple piece of angle iron with one hole through the top for the bolt to hold the cylinder end and multiple holes to mount the bracket to the door. If the door's sheet metal is weak, using a backing plate behind the sheet metal becomes necessary. This helps to distribute the force over a wider area, making the door a little stronger.

The dash mount is a harder hurdle to overcome. Blandford suggests starting with a piece of round stock that you've drilled and tapped to mount the other end of the cylinder. Next, he would weld this round stock to the largest piece of steel he could fit under the dash.

"If the dash itself has no good supports, it will be necessary to cross-brace this bracket," he says. "Normally, the dash will have at least one brace that runs from the center console over to the door pillar. If this isn't very beefy, plan on running at least two brackets from your cylinder mount over to the firewall."

He also notes that in a typical hydraulic door setup, you will have 200 to 300 pounds of force at these cylinder mounting points, so he recommends bolting the mounts as opposed to welding them. "If you're wrong on your placement, it's a little easier to move something if it has been bolted," he says.

The front door cylinder in place, attached between the dash and door mounts. *Freedom Motors, USA*

Now it's time for the tricky part: figuring the exact location of your mounts. This is much easier to do with the help of a friend, Blandford says, adding, "Although I have, in a pinch, used my friend duct tape." Start by bolting your dash mount to your cylinder and have your friend hold the cylinder in place under the dash. With the door closed, hold or tape the door mount in such a way that it lines up with the rod end of your cylinder fully closed. Then open the door, pull out the rod end of the cylinder, and check to see if it still lines up with the mount.

"A little long is OK, as it's almost impossible to get the right stroke to line up exactly," Blandford says. "If it's a little short of the mount, that means either the door will not open all the way when the cylinder is extended, or you'll need to move the mount closer to the hinge, thus using a shorter stroke to open the door. Just remember, the closer you are to the hinge point, the more force it will take to close the door. This is a leverage thing. The further out on the door you are, the less leverage it takes to close."

From here, follow these two steps:

With the door closed and the cylinder collapsed, move the hole on the door mount in or out until it lines up with the cylinder.

Top: Cylinders with a variety of different bores and strokes, as well as different mounting ends. *Freedom Motors, USA*

Right: A typical double pump–mounting bracket. *Freedom Motors, USA*

With the door open and the cylinder fully extended, move the door mount in or out on the door to get the cylinder lined up with your hole.

Repeat these two steps until you have a location that works for both the open and the closed position. Then securely attach both mounts and bolt the cylinder to the mounts.

Next, determine where you want to mount your pump. Blandford suggests mounting it inside the vehicle because if it is on the outside, the pump will be subject to road debris and you'll have to route the hydraulic lines through the vehicle floor or firewall.

"An acceptable location would be the trunk of a car, or behind an interior panel in the case of a van or SUV," Blandford adds. "Stay away from under the hood, as excessive heat from the motor could have an effect on some materials used in the hydraulic lines."

After mounting the pump, run your lines from the pump to the cylinder. Then fill the pump with fluid and follow the pump's instructions to bleed all the air from the system. Bleed the system with the cylinder bolted to the dash but not to the door, Blandford says, so that if something goes horribly wrong, it won't wrench your door from its hinges.

"This next step is really important," he adds. "I only use as much pressure as necessary to open and close the door. Since I'm able to adjust pressure in both directions, I can set the open pressure, then set the close pressure. These two values will usually be different, as it takes a bit more pressure to close a vehicle door." In fact, modern vehicles are so airtight that you can actually feel the air being pushed as the door closes, making it necessary to slightly increase the closing pressure in an effort to overcome that air.

Blandford suggests making the pump accessible so that you can make the pump pressure adjustments easily.

"I'll start with the pressure backed way off and attach the rod end of the cylinder to the door. I'll run the pump and see what happens," he says. "If the door doesn't move, I up the pressure. I'll do this in both directions, and only give it enough pressure to make it open and close securely. Once set, I will pull the pump out of the vehicle and run it on a bench with pressure gauges attached to the pump to see what I actually ended up with. I'm checking to make sure I'm running the system within all component specs, so as not to overpressurize the system."

If he has more room to push, he makes a note of the pressures required for the job, then adds 50 to 100 pounds of pressure to those figures so that the system will work in all types of situations—warm weather, cold weather, well-charged battery, weak battery.

Going, going, gone. This vehicle has three separate actions—gull door, ramp, and front door—all running off just one pump. It's triggered through one handheld two-button remote control. *Freedom Motors, USA*

"If you built your mounts securely enough, the slight increase in pressure will have no noticeable effect on the vehicle," Blandford says. "Plus, it's a good idea to make note of your operating pressure in case you have to duplicate your work for someone else."

Is That All?

There are two more important points to remember when it comes to working with a hydraulic-operated door: One, that door we just moved with hydraulics needs somehow to be unlatched before the hydraulics can actually open it. Two, we have a pump and a cylinder hooked up that can open and close the door, but how do we actually control the pump?

First, let's tackle unlatching the door. Several companies make aftermarket door solenoids that will unlatch a door. The best place to buy one of these aftermarket parts is not at your local auto supply store—it's better to go to a car stereo shop.

Second, you have to figure out how to control the pump. You can use something as simple as a switch mounted somewhere on the vehicle. But that option requires the switch to be on the outside of the vehicle, so you can actually get inside it by pushing the switch and activating the hydraulic door. A slicker approach is to use a set of remote controls to trigger some relays installed in the vehicle to run the pump.

"The pumps I use normally draw about 20 to 25 amps, while the solenoids to unlatch the doors draw about 13 to 15 amps," Blandford says. "I will use a bank of relays soldered together to form the control unit and break the unit up into an 'open' circuit and a 'close' circuit. I also always make sure the relays are capable of handling the current draw. [You need to] think about what is needed for the 'open' circuit to work, and using simple relay logic, draw out your diagram."

He likes to break up the power supply needed by the control unit as well, using a fuse block. That way, if one thing fails on the system, not everything will necessarily fail.

"Plus, it makes it easier to track down a problem if you know what fuse you are blowing all the time," he says. "I use fuses as opposed to circuit breakers because if you are having a problem and a fuse blows, that circuit is now dead, alerting you to a possible problem. A lot of the circuit breakers will automatically reset, sometimes hiding a problem until it is too late."

As far as which remote control to use, talk to your local stereo shop guys about getting a system that is capable of outputting two momentary signals. One signal can be used to open everything and the other to close everything. The reason Blandford likes using momentary signals is that they are only active while you are activating the remote, thus giving you some control over how long the system runs. This can be an important safety feature, especially if you realize someone still has his or her fingers in the doorway as it begins to close.

What Kind of Components Should You Use?

Here are the parts Blandford recommends if you want to take on a hydraulics project. (Keep in mind most of his work revolves around the automotive industry; he has automated front doors, gull doors, rear hatches, and ramps on a variety of vehicles. This specialization has allowed him to narrow down what he needs to use.)

- **Pumps:** He normally uses one single pump that's capable of pressures in excess of 2,000 psi, with a flow rate of about a gallon a minute. He favors a bidirectional unit that allows him to control the pressure in both directions independently. He also likes a pump that is compact in size.

- **Cylinders:** The cylinders Blandford uses are usually a $7/8$- to $1 1/8$-inch bore, which give a good compromise between power and speed when used with the above pump. Some standard strokes are 6 inches for front doors, 9 inches for rear hatches, and 14 inches for doors that open past 90 degrees.

- **Control units:** Blandford makes his control units using standard DPDT relays. "This allows flexibility when designing a new system," he says. "I can control one or two pumps, up to three different door solenoids, and can even roll down one window to relieve air pressure and roll it back up again. All control is operated through a two-channel remote system."

Pneumatics

**"With air, there's no oil all over the place."
— Eric Scarlett**

Pneumatic operating systems work very similarly to hydraulic systems, with the essential difference being that pneumatics involve the use of compressed air rather than hydraulic fluid to move whatever it is that needs moving.

Eric Scarlett, a seasoned expert in working with pneumatics, has tackled many air bag installations as owner of First Class Autowerks. He advises that even a pretty seasoned at-home fabricator leave air bag installations to an experienced professional due to the fact that the suspension system in your car or truck is critical to the safety of the vehicle.

"If it's done right, air bag suspension maintains itself, maintains its own pressure of air at all times," Scarlett says. "A lot of people make air bag kits that they claim bolt right into your car. Nothing bolts right into your car. People can say whatever they want, but when you put an air ride suspension system on your car, that is customizing your car. It's custom fitted to your car, not like the stuff that comes in a kit. For instance, take the fittings they give you; they usually have nylon quick-change ends. Put them under enough pressure and they break, they crack, they leak, they're garbage."

Another factor to consider when using pneumatics in automotive systems is that they run on compressed air, which causes condensation and eventually water and rust to metal parts.

"Some people want chrome [pneumatic] tanks because they look cool, but I don't put chrome tanks in a car. I have my tanks coated on the inside to prevent rust," Scarlett says. "When rust gets into the system, it screws up the valves and the next thing you know you're driving down the freeway and your car slowly starts dropping down and starts scraping; or you park somewhere and when you come back to the car it's lowered on one side.

"Air suspension is serious stuff," he adds. "Before you let anyone install a system in your car, talk to other people they've worked for; go into their shop and check out the quality of their work. If it's done wrong and malfunctions while you're going down the freeway at 70 miles per hour, it can kill you, and maybe some other people, too. In my shop, if you can't do it right the first time, then don't do it at all."

The following photos in this section illustrate the highlights of a typical First Class Autowerks air bag installation, this one on a 1981 Chevy pickup.

Right: Rear half of the truck with the C-notch, which allows the truck to sit lower, already installed.

Left: The valves in place. Two valves are needed for each air bag. The installation also includes a sliver digital air-pressure sender.

The air bag mounts and spider-like crossmembers that hold the mounts in place. Also seen are the four-link bars that hold the axle in place.

The air compressors mounted under the engine compartment.

Front A-arms with the bag in place, lower A-arm plated, and modified upper shock mount.

The air tank mounted on the side of the frame.

The stock gas tank and axle.

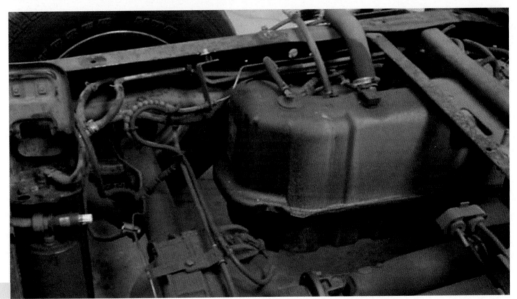

The truck bed with sections cut out before the bed has been dropped and the sections welded together.

Here are the metal flames and bowtie that will be welded to the truck bed.

The truck bed after application of a bed liner.

The completed truck lowered for its first ride.

MEET THE PROS

Todd Blandford

"Be leery of self-proclaimed masters."

Todd Blandford is the owner of Great Lakes Custom Creations. He has been involved in "hydros" for the past 16 years, primarily in the handicapped transportation industry. In fact, he developed a system that uses custom-built control units with smaller-sized cylinders and pumps that react faster than the standard units, which are presently commercially available. His path to this type of work began when he was a teenager in Michigan.

"My fascination with things mechanical and cars in general began at the age of 17 when I purchased my first automobile, a lime-green AMC Gremlin," Blandford says. "Shade-tree mechanics started immediately following the purchase. I replaced a front wheel bearing before I

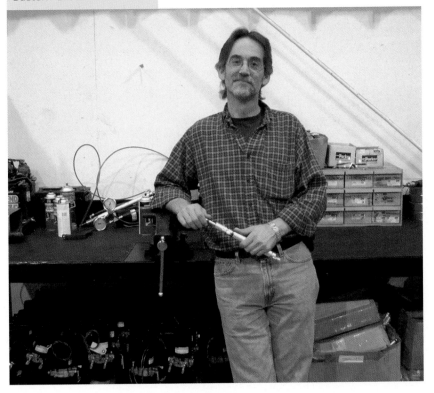

Todd Blandford knows his way around hydraulics installations. *Great Lakes Custom Creations*

ever knew what one was, or even what its purpose was; living with the Michigan winters, bodywork followed shortly after."

After a few years spent managing restaurants, Blandford applied for a job with a company that installed hydraulic systems into handicapped adapted vehicles.

"The interview went poorly, but somehow I managed to land the job anyway," he says. "Great, I thought. I had no tools, hadn't worked on a car in years, and knew absolutely nothing about hydraulics—fun times those first few months. Over the next few years, I kept my mouth shut, my eyes open, and managed to learn enough to make myself useful.

"Through trial and error, I learned what worked and what didn't, what components were best suited to what applications. I learned to weld, how to break and shear sheet metal, how to fabricate. I prototyped, refined, reworked every aspect of the system, all in an effort to provide maximum reliability for minimum complexity. I spent many long hours on the road reworking previously modified vehicles, often in bad weather, lying in driveways in the dark. But all it took was the smile on the face of the end user to make it all worthwhile."

By 2003, Blandford had become a hydraulics expert. Blandford says the hydraulic professionals out there often use their own methods, products, and practices, so he recommends that anyone contemplating a hydraulic installation should get a second opinion about their project.

PLASTICS

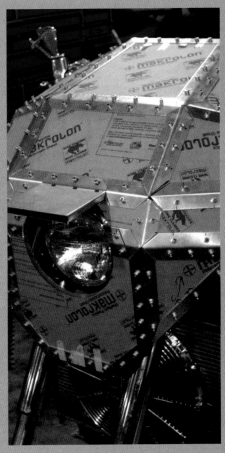

Plastic is defined as giving shape or form to substance. How you give it substance is the focus of this chapter.

"Working with a high-tech polycarbonate [plastic] is basically like working with wood. You can use regular wood tools like a table saw; you can drill it, tap it, hit it with a sledgehammer, and you won't break it."
— Eddie Paul, Hollywood car builder

Plastics are man-made synthetics that, in certain chemical combinations, can rival the strength of the strongest steels, yet when heated can be shaped, cut, welded, formed, sanded, and painted to the point they appear to be made of something else entirely—making plastics a great choice when fabricating a custom project.

Not only are the tools needed to work with most plastics essentially the same as those used in woodworking—skill saws, handsaws, sanders, drills, etc.—so are the skills required to use them. Tools that are more specifically necessary when working with plastics include handheld heat guns, die grinders, and paint spray guns. None of these tools requires anything additional in the way of shop space, lighting, or ventilation, so if you have a shop set up for woodworking, you are ready for "plastic working," too.

There is one item, however, that you should get if you really plan to do a lot of plastic fabrication. It is what Hollywood car builder Eddie Paul calls one of his most favorite tools: a vacuum forming machine. You can find plans on the Internet to construct this type of machine, which can give the home fabricator the ability to make colored, textured, or clear plastics. Most of these machines can be built for less than $300.

Plastic may also be formed into various shapes using a portable shop furnace or a simple and inexpensive electric furnace operating in a range of about 250 to 400 degrees Fahrenheit.

In Paul's experience, where he's built not only cars for movie sets, but various machine-related props as well, he has worked with almost every kind of plastic out there. For one such job, he used multiple plastics and standard home tools on one prop.

"The prop's parts ended up being vacuum formed over wooden plugs, rough cut with an electric chainsaw, ground down with a disc grinder, then sanded with a belt sander," he says. "Most of the wood plugs were not even all that smooth. My crew had never used plastic before so the skill level was minimal, to say the least. But the project was completed on time and, after a little paint, it looked like a showpiece; in fact, it was a showpiece."

A Shark Tale: Take One

Paul compares building a great white shark to building a nuclear-powered sub or a supercomputer—none of these being an easy task. But just like any job, you start with a plan or blueprint and a list of materials.

"Long ago I learned a lesson that Isaac Newton once learned from Descartes: When a problem seems too large and complicated, break it down into small problems and solve each of them individually," Paul says. "So I broke the shark down into basic problems (bite-size projects), such as, first, what will I make it out of? Well, it would be used in the ocean, so the materials would need to be noncorrosives such as stainless steel, plastic, brass, and/or anodized aluminum."

Next, Paul says, he considered weight. He didn't want to create an expensive anchor, so that led him to think about making the shark out of plastic materials. He decided to cast the skin out of a relatively new polycarbonate product, then add micro balloons to boost the shark's buoyancy.

The beast's size, however, proved to be a tougher decision. "All the sharks we had previously tried to film were about 5 to 6 feet long," Paul says. "My assumption was that since the background of the expected shot was to be blue water, I could cheat the shot and use a smaller shark. This would save time and money, as there would be no reference for size. I decided to make the shark 18 inches long, small enough to handle but large enough to showcase some detail."

That decision wasn't in line with the client's. "When I proudly showed them my little work of art, I was a bit set back by the response. They said, 'This looks wonderful. When will ours be done?'"

Realizing that the client probably wanted something larger, Paul questioned them as to how much bigger they wanted the shark to be. "'How about 10 feet?" the client responded. "We don't want it too large!"

Take Two: Back to the Drawing Board

From there, Paul created a full set of templates based on a larger design and transferred them to plastic. He also tweaked the design further so that it would retain its ability to float. This included redesigning the shark's vertebrae into flat, 1-inch-wide strips of polycarbonate. These were fastened to the top and bottom of the silhouette's center spar with brackets allowing them to bow outward.

"These 'ribs' were attached within a few days, and the body looked like a real shark body, minus the head," Paul says. "As soon as the head was complete, it was attached with angle brackets."

Paul says the shark's hollowed-out fiberglass head was then rough-sculpted from foam and coated with fiberglass and a layer of body putty. From there, the details on the head were carved and sanded into the body filler before a mold was cast. Then the mold was sprayed with mold release and a fiberglass head was cast inside it.

"The new head was pulled out and set aside for painting and detail: eyes, teeth, gums, and airbrushing," Paul says. "Neither my dad nor my then-girlfriend (now my wife) Renée escaped the great

Computer-generated image uses grid to ensure all parts are designed to scale.

THE MARAUDER
Great White Shark Submarine
Length................12 ft.
Width..................6 ft.
Height.................5 ft.
Weight (approx).200 lbs.
©2003 E.P. Industries

THE MARAUDER

white's vengeance. They were both drafted on sight into the hard labor of shaping and sanding the body and cutting the thousands of feet of polycarbonate sheet that went into making the monster. [Yet] it wasn't until we started casting the skin that life took an evil turn. When I needed it to be stiff, it was flexible; when I wanted it flexible, it was rigid. The second and third skins were better but not right. The fourth skin was the one I used."

Once the skin was complete and painted, it was installed on the skeleton and the shark earned its name: Allison. Then she was shipped off.

When it finally reached its destination, as did Paul, the time came to test Allison's abilities. Paul went down in the water with her, as did Mark Blessington, a longtime diver.

"It would have been difficult to do alone because I needed to take the shark down to about 30 feet and balance her out by adding weight through the mouth," Paul says. "The weights were hung onto a cable that allowed me to pull her weight forward or rearward with a simple pulley system. The whole process took about 45 minutes, and the shark was balanced perfectly.

"The next morning, we put Allison back into the water and started filming the whites interacting with her. I had her set up so that I could operate her from a shark cage in the water. This way, I had a clear view of the area and could steer her around. Her range was limited only by the 50-foot umbilical that carried her air and allowed her motion. She looked right at home as about five or six sharks joined in to swim along with her."

To get more action for the film Paul's clients were making, they decided to make Allison look like a dying shark. "I moved a small weight onto one of the pectorals and moved the control stick in an erratic motion," Paul says. "It was as if someone had turned on a switch and run high voltage through the ocean. The sharks took on a different air, one of danger.

"It didn't take long for the first attack by the biggest of the sharks. I saw her swim directly at Allison's right-side [starboard] gill area and slowly but steadily take a large bite out of the plastic-and-rubber shark. She did this four more times, and within minutes my robo-shark was reduced to an expensive gutted toy. But, most important of all, we had gotten the needed shot with my reputation still intact."

For an encore, Eddie Paul decided to build a more complex great white, this one large enough in fact to carry a diver/driver inside.

Sushi 1 nearing completion. *Eddie Paul Industries*

Sushi 1 ready for a test.
Eddie Paul Industries

Take Three: A Bigger and Badder Shark

The third shark, dubbed Sushi 1 by Eddie Paul's daughter, Ariel, ended up being a bigger and badder shark at 14 feet long and 4.6 feet tall with a diameter of 54 inches. It not only needed to look as much as possible like a real shark, but also had to be large enough for a diver/operator and be self-powered, swimming by tail motion.

The other requirements:

- It had to have a method of entry and exit that could be operated from the inside and outside.
- It had to be neutrally buoyant with the ability to become positive or negatively buoyant when needed by the enclosed operator (pilot).
- It needed to be simple to operate and repair (in the field) and simple to load and unload in water.
- It had to be constructed from noncorrosive materials and produce no

sound or electrical discharges.
- The operator would need to use a rebreather unit and must have the ability to navigate open water in a reasonable manner.
- It needed to be air-powered but not expel air bubbles.
- It needed to have reasonable duration while submerged, with the pilot able to communicate with the support crew.
- The air system had to be easy to replace and there would be a video link to the outside for the ability to navigate in open water.
- Of course, all this had to be accomplished within a few months and for less than $100,000.

The process behind the project is detailed below.

Construction of the Plug and Mold

"We researched the great white, comparing photos and film of the shark from all angles, then compiled a rendered image of the shark on 3-D studio MAX for pulling off dimensions," Paul says.

"This was converted to a DXF file and brought into AutoCAD for dimensional extrapolation. The 3-D image was converted into a top, side, and end view."

From that profile, he built a rotary fixture with 2-inch steel tubing that was about 48 inches wide and about 20 feet long. This tube was to be the center reinforcement tube for the shark and had bearings on each end, allowing it to be rotated. Then 2-inch-thick by 4 x 8-foot foam blocks were glued to this tube with foam glue spray. After that was complete, Paul rough cut the foam blocks to the silhouette of the shark by increasing the AutoCAD drawing to full scale.

"Successive layers were then added. With each block of foam or layer of sprayed foam, we would start with chainsaws and progressively convert to finer methods of sculpting until we were down to sandpaper-wrapped toothpicks," Paul says. "This process went on for about three weeks until the plug was complete and ready to be coated in preparation for the fiberglass molding process, after which it went out to a fiberglass company who shot the mold perfectly."

Skin

The shark's skin needed to be flexible, strong, naturally buoyant, and easy to work with, so Paul decided to use a brush-applicable transparent urethane two-part elastomer that set up in about 10 minutes. The shark required three and a half kits of the elastomer at a total weight of 67 pounds per kit.

Power

Paul says he chose to use pneumatic power in the shark because it could be used directly in saltwater without costly waterproof housings, and is readily available.

"It can be recharged in minutes while at sea by simply changing the scuba bottle," he adds, noting that he even used a newer scuba tank that contained 140

Sushi 1 was amazingly lifelike in the water. *Eddie Paul Industries*

cubic feet of air at 3,400 psi. "This opened up a more practical approach to air power; this tank is basically compressed horsepower on tap."

Control

"If simple is better, our controls could not be simpler," Paul notes. "A single joystick was mounted in the rear portion of the head (which tilts forward on hinges to allow entry). As the head tilted forward, the single stick control tilted forward with it. This was done for added clearance and ease of entry to the shark, feet first."

Once the pilot entered the shark body, he or she could tilt the head up (closing it) and lock it shut by toggling the controls onto the second rib back, near the front upper spine area.

"This placed the control valve and control stick in front of, and slightly to the right of, the pilot," Paul says. "Then, by moving the control stick to the right, the tail moves to the right and moving it left moves the tail left. A single tail stroke moves the shark forward about 36 inches. Each successive stroke provides forward thrust of an equal amount."

Turning

Paul's shark can be turned by the same control stick and a technique of timed movements of the stick. For instance, if you move the stick to the left for two seconds, the shark's tail will move left a full stroke. If you move the control stick to the right for one second, the tail moves right about one-half the distance. "Repeating this motion will allow the tail to act as a power device and a rudder," Paul says.

Buoyancy

To increase buoyancy, a weight was added below the shark's center of gravity to help stabilize it and keep it oriented in the upright position. To increase the safety factor, a secondary inflatable buoyancy system [SIBS] was added.

"These SIBS can be deployed [inflated] on command and will be utilized for emergency ascents only," Paul says. "[The inflation of] one or two of these bags should easily bring the shark up at a reasonable rate of ascent."

Vision and Navigation

Navigation proved to be a bit more complicated than expected, Paul admits, because there was no sensory feedback from the outside water. "You are basically in a sealed shark with no water flow indicating either speed or direction, meaning that the pilot had no way of perceiving speed, movement, or even direction. I would often imagine a failed swim only to come out of the shark to a jubilant crew of onlookers seeing the success of the swim," he says.

Eventually, he installed a video camera and monitor system that would give the driver a look at how the swim was going.

Needless to say, the great white did its thing, giving audiences an unprecedented look at these deadly creatures in their natural environment.

After all that work, one really has to wonder how a kid who dropped out of high school and started out working on cars and choppers in his garage ended up as, well, as Eddie Paul.

"My dad was a metal fabricator; he did cars and sheet metal work," Paul says. "He taught me to weld when I was about 12. I made my first mini-bike at 12 or 13. He gave me a car to customize before I was old enough to drive."

Now, more than 25 years after breaking into Hollywood, Eddie Paul is still making cars for the movies. He's worked on more than 100 films to date and, while some things have changed, it's still basically a 24/7 operation with deadlines that would make most people crazy. For one film, his shop needed to build 220 cars in a month. Needless to say, they got 'em done.

For those of you getting ready to set up shop to do your own metal shaping work, Paul has some words of advice. The first thing he recommends is considering your power source.

"Everyone has 110 AC," he says. "If you also have a 220 AC line, so much the better, but you don't need one to get started. You're also going to need a good welder. There are a number of choices, including an arc, MIG, TIG, and a number of subcategories for each of them. But if you're going to be working on normal cars made of sheet metal, you can get by with a 110 MIG machine that can be run off of a small generator or any 110 outlet.

"Most MIGs are around 100 amps and are good for 1/4-inch steel, which is fine for most automotive work. They can be bought for about $300 to $400."

The biggest mistake beginners make with a MIG is to pull the gun during the weld when it should be pushed, Paul says, adding that only practice will help you get that down.

Another great tool he recommends getting is a plasma cutter.

"They aren't cheap, but you'll find that with a bit of practice you'll be cutting metal like it was paper," he says. "If you use a piece of scrap iron or aluminum as a guide, you'll cut a line that looks like the metal was sheared off. You'll also want some of the standard manual cutting tools like shears, snips, an air hammer with cutting heads, cutting wheels, nibblers, saws, and so on."

Like our other expert fabricators, Paul's own list of tools and equipment (of which the above is only a small sample) reflects the myriad of different projects he has been involved in over the years. And, like most fabricators, you will probably find yourself buying more tools and equipment in order to do more varied jobs.

Paul's final piece of advice is simple: While you're waiting for the guy with the suitcase full of money to arrive, use the time to practice, practice, practice.

OUT IN THE GARAGE

MAKING A MAKROLON WINDSHIELD

Before delving into the construction of the ultimate great white, let's take a look at the way Eddie Paul used Makrolon (a polycarbonate plastic) in a project that has applications for a lot of home fabricators: a motorcycle windshield.

"Makrolon is great stuff to work with, a dream material," Paul says. "It's lighter than glass—doesn't corrode, doesn't rot; you put Makrolon windows in your house, nobody will ever break in that way. They even have some now that are scratch-resistant. The safety shields in my shop are made of it."

Of course, there are things to keep in mind when you're working with Makrolon. You can't weld it because it has moisture in it, which will cause bubbles to form in the plastic. "But it can be vacuum formed," Paul says. "You could make a whole car out of it if you wanted to."

1: One of the first steps in the windshield project is to lay out the pattern on a piece of foam core cardboard so you can cut it and place it on the vehicle for fitting. You can cut foam core with a razor blade, and it's strong enough to be taped in place.

2: This section is over the headlight and fairly simple to make. Paul always starts with the center section of a design and works his way outward so the parts will stay symmetrical.

3: Measure the rest of the parts and mark the outside dimensions for laying out a pattern.

4: Use a compass to triangulate a point by bisecting two arcs. You may need to brush up on your basic geometry for this task, but this is the best way to find a point on a flat plane.

5: A few pieces are now in place and the windshield is already starting to take on a nice shape, even though it is composed of nothing but flat pieces.

6: With the patterns in place, test the windshield to make sure it can turn properly without hitting the frame. This is the time to trim if needed.

7: Cut the first parts from the high-tech polycarbonate and lay them out to see how well they will fit with the aluminum brackets.

8: This is the point when things can get frustrating. Add one piece of aluminum trim at a time, drilling the holes to mount it to one piece of Makrolon, then removing it to mark it for the next piece of Makrolon.

9: Each time you add a new piece of Makrolon, you have to mark and drill the aluminum trim, then reinstall it for marking of the contiguous panel. You must also mark and trim the angles to match between the panels. Paul likes to leave the paper on the high-tech polycarbonate so that he can avoid having to mask it during the paint job.

10

10: The windshield is now in place and bolted up. This project required more than 100 bolts and 200 washers. Adding the headlight cover is the next step.

11: It requires a bit of skill to make sure all of the angles fit perfectly. The fun part of this project was painting the bike with a camouflage theme, which required a bit of airbrush work.

11

12: The windshield is unmasked and ready to mount. The headlight cover is then added to the front lower section. This little puppy weighed in at almost 50 pounds, but it will go a long way in stopping a bullet.

13: All the parts are now coming together. Without a good pattern, making this windshield could be a geometric nightmare.

14: The finished Boss Hoss Secret Weapon is ready to rumble with the best of them, and yes, that is a 350 Chevy in there.

15: As seen from the front, the Secret Weapon can stop traffic without even firing a shot from its (fake) twin guns.

MEET THE PROS

Eddie Paul

"I always look for challenges."

The fact that Eddie Paul was chosen as our final master fabricator (Makrolon Windshield project, pages 146-153) makes perfect sense as his great white shark project actually encompassed all of the previous fabrication processes featured in this book. Designing and constructing the final shark involved AutoCAD computer technology, complex sheet metal work, MIG and TIG welding, precision machining, fiberglass molds, plastic fabrication, and pneumatics.

Even though this book is about how to fabricate damn near anything, most home fabricators reading this probably never thought that a great white shark would be included under the "anything"

umbrella. Well, we couldn't let that happen, could we?

For master fabricator and inventor Eddie Paul, his life has been full of fascinating jobs. In the late 1960s, Paul started chopping motorcycles out of his garage. When he moved into his own studio to continue his chopper building, his third customer was someone from a movie studio.

"The guy said he was working on a movie called *Grease*, and the studio was in a real bind because they needed 48 cars. So, this guy says to me, 'If you can do it, this is yours.'"

Of course, Paul didn't have many guys working for him back in those days, so he had to go out and hire more off the street.

"Then I jumped on the phone and bought all the cars I could find from the 1940s and '50s, no matter what condition

Bottom Left: Eddie Paul has fabricated nearly anything and everything under the sun, from movie cars and custom motorcycles to mechanical sharks. *Eddie Paul Industries*

Bottom Right: The Strata-Cycle, which Eddie Paul built in two weeks for the Rangers. It is an example of thermal-forming plastic in its highest form. "The plugs that we formed over were made from wood, and the plastics were a combination of ABS, PVC, and clear and tinted acrylics," Paul says. "The bike is now about 10 years old and still looks the way it did the day we built it." *Eddie Paul Industries*

The shark being tested in the water. *Eddie Paul Industries*

Left: Three Eddie Paul prototypes. *Eddie Paul Industries*

Right Top: A close-up look at the inner workings of the shark Paul created for movie-making magic. *Eddie Paul Industries*

Right Bottom: Filming action.

they were in, put a sleeping bag next to my desk, and worked around the clock until it was done," he says. "I think we finished the last car with about five minutes to spare. From that point on there was no worry about the next month's rent."

Now the movies he's provided cars for include *The Fast and the Furious* trilogy, *xXx*, and *Taxi*. His fabrication projects have also included re-creating antique flying machines, making miniature submarines, constructing lightweight portable pumping equipment for fire departments, and airborne laser weapon systems.

But even for Eddie Paul, who has had more than his share of difficult and unusual projects in the past, constructing a great white shark proved to be one of his greatest challenges. The shark, or sharks (as there were ultimately three), had to be able to swim in the ocean, perform on cue for a camera crew, and fool the real great whites it would be swimming with.

MEET THE PROS

Dwaine Jungen

"To be experienced, you need to experience life's lessons."

For future off-road fabrication maestro Dwaine Jungen, the career journey began, as it so often does, by following in the footsteps of others, in his case as his father's "tool-go-fer" on various projects. As a youth, Jungen hauled junked parts home in his wagon to be, as he puts it, "dissected and scattered," then loaded into Dad's company truck and hauled off to the dump. "The turning point," he says, "was when I learned to reassemble and make the junk work. I sold quite a few 'repaired' lawnmowers."

Jungen counts his father Bill, Uncle Tom, and select others as his mentors and teachers in things mechanical and life in general.

"All of my training has come from life lessons at the 'school of hard knocks,'" he says. "I graduated in the top of my class in high school and turned down a college scholarship because I wanted to be an engine builder. A college education is important, but it's not necessarily for everyone. College does not teach talent, ability, or desire, the way it can be learned by living."

For Dwaine Jungen, the DARPA Challenge is an unexpected adventure. Whether the Scorpion-Fox wins the $2 million or not, you can bet it won't be the end of the story.

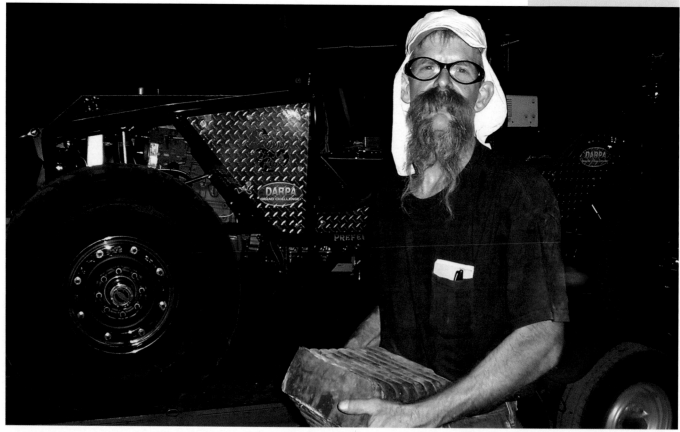

Jungen's company, Preferred Chassis Fabrication Inc., is the owner and manufacturer of the Scorpion off-road vehicle—a remarkable machine that can cope with just about any terrain it traverses. For the past year, he has been working with the Center for Applied Research & Technology (CART) to design and construct the Scorpion-Fox, an unmanned, robotic version of the vehicle built expressly to compete in the 2005 $2 million DARPA Challenge. Sponsored by the Department of Defense's Defense Advanced Research Projects Agency (DARPA), the DARPA Challenge vehicles must cover a 175-mile course through rugged desert terrain guided only by their on-board computer systems.

Here are specifications for the Scorpion-Fox that Jungen has created:

- **chassis**: fabricated .125-inch wall DOM tubing
- **length:** 150 inches
- **width:** 80 inches
- **height:** 61 to 73 inches, variable
- **engine:** 4BT-3.9, 4-cylinder diesel
- **transmission:** Team RAMCO built, GM 700-R4
- **transfer case:** advanced adapters; 2, 4.3 gear ratio
- **drivelines:** Tom Woods custom
- **axles:** 4:10 gear ratio with ARB differentials

- **wheels/tires:** mil spec bead lock/16/ 38.5 x 16.5
- **shocks:** Bilstein 7100
- **suspension:** Scorpion air
- **brakes:** actuated 4-wheel vented disc
- **steering:** dual power with electronic control
- **throttle control:** electronic
- **power options:** pure sine inverter
- **air system:** dual air systems
- **control interface:** AV power products/Preferred Chassis Fabrication (supplies control power and sensor monitoring and enables vehicle functions to be controlled through RS232 communication links)
- **sensor array:** Center for Applied Research and Technology (180-degree field of view and 90-degree field of view laser measurement sensors, vehicle guidance system, global positioning system, and stereoscopic cameras)
- **navigation system:** Center for Applied Research and Technology (four Pentium processors, cabled networking hub, and the intelligence of the autonomy control program)

"Through desire, the love of what I do, and the help of many skilled people willing to share their talents, I've been able to have the success I have today," Jungen says.

The Scorpion-Fox: Ready to rumble.

Index